TH
BASIC
COMMU
INFORM
WORK

THE
BASICS OF
COMMUNITY
INFORMATION
WORK

ALLAN BUNCH
Library Manager (Peterborough Area),
Cambridgeshire Libraries

Library Association Publishing
London

© Allan Bunch 1984, 1993

Published by
Library Association Publihsing Ltd
7 Ridgmount Street
London WC1E 7AE

First published 1984 as *The basics of information work*
This second edition 1993

British Library Cataloguing in Publication Data

Bunch, Allan
　　Basics of Community Information Work. —
　　2Rev.ed
　　I. Title
　　361.06

　　ISBN 1-85604-038-0

Typeset from author's disk in 10/12pt Times by Library Association Publishing Ltd
Printed and made in Great Britain by Bookcraft (Bath) Ltd

Contents

Introduction   vii

1 Who needs an information service?   1

2 Setting up the service   16

3 Staffing   42

4 The information base   56

5 Giving out information   84

6 Publicity and promotion   114

7 How to maintain an effective service   129

8 Using computers   140

Further reading   159

Appendix 1 Model job specification for the organizer of an information service   161

Appendix 2 List of umbrella organizations covering community information and advice services   165

Index of works cited   167

General index   170

This is the second edition of a book originally entitled *Basics of information work*. The move from this general title to the more specific one of 'community information' merely reflects the true nature of the book even in its first edition. However, the principles are the same, whatever kind of information service you are planning to set up, and it is mainly the examples that are relevant to the area of community information. For this second edition I have expanded the section on staffing into a full chapter, added an additional chapter on the use of computers in community information work, and generally updated booklists, addresses, etc.

The book is one of a series and is intended to provide a basic introduction to its subject. It is aimed both at library staff who are interested in extending the scope of an existing reference service to meet special needs in the community and at those who are called upon to set up or operate a community information service but have no training in librarianship or experience of information-handling skills. In trying to cater for these two groups, the book runs the risk of not satisfying either by being too elementary or too complicated. I have tried to overcome this by including both cheap and simple solutions as well as more complicated and extensive ones, and by indicating further sources of information.

The text is based largely on my own experience of setting up community information services in Peterborough, and many of the examples are drawn from local material. This is not to imply that these are the only or the best examples; indeed there are many such services in existence doing excellent work. It was simply a matter of convenience to use material at hand rather than spend time searching for it. However, I am grateful to Nigel Graves of Camden Community Information Services for permission to reproduce examples from the excellent material his service produces.

This book is essentially a practical manual aimed at those who want to respond to an identified need in their community. It does not attempt to delve into the history or philosophy of community information, as these are more appropriately subjects of academic study.

Nevertheless, holding firm to the principle that the proverbial man or woman on the Clapham omnibus reading this book ought to understand what it is about, I feel the need at least to define 'community information'. I can do no better than wheel out a couple of definitions I have used on numerous occasions in other writings. The first, and one of the earliest, is by an American librarian, Joseph C. Donohue, who termed it as information needed to cope with 'crises in the lives of individuals and communities'.[1] Donohue expanded on this definition by identifying two types of information provided by a community information service:

1 *survival information* such as that related to health, housing, income, legal protection, economic opportunity, political rights, etc.;
2 *citizen action information*, needed for effective participation as individuals or as members of a group in the social, political, legal, economic process.[2]

The other definition occurs in *Community information: what libraries can do*, the report of the Library Association Working Party on Community Information, which identified community information services as those which 'assist individuals and groups with daily problem-solving and with participation in the democratic process. The services concentrate on the needs of those who do not have ready access to other sources of assistance and on the most important problems that people have to face, problems to do with their homes, their jobs and their rights.'[3]

References

1 Donohue, Joseph C., 'Community information services – a proposed definition'. *In* Martin, S. K., *Community information politics. Proceedings 39th ASIS annual meeting.* Vol. 13, American Society for Information Science, 1976, fiche 8, frame E4.
2 ibid. fiche 9, frame B12.
3 *Community information services: what libraries can do,* Library Asociation, 1980, 12.

Chapter One

Who needs an information service?

Many organizations, from national campaigning bodies to local tenants' groups, from time to time identify a need to set up an information service to meet the requirements of the following:

- their own staff or membership;
- the general public, as a whole or belonging to a defined geographical area;
- sections of the public with particular needs, such as disabled or elderly people;
- workers and public associated with a particular purpose, e.g. a redevelopment scheme or anti-dampness campaign.

It may sound obvious to state that, before setting up an information service, you should ask yourself, first of all, some very basic questions – like those a journalist asks when writing a story: who?, what?, when?, where?, why?, and how? – but not necessarily in that order. Surprisingly, there are many instances where these questions have not been asked and services have been set up which were either not wanted, the wrong type of service to meet clients' needs, a duplication of already existing services, too ambitious for available staffing or resources, or lacking in commitment from the organization's management or staff.

The moral is that careful thought and preparation at the outset can save a lot of wasted effort and be the sound foundation on which to build a successful service. It is always better to start modestly and grow, than to be too ambitious and have to retract or fail completely. This book tries to follow the same principle in the way its information is presented, moving from simple, cheap solutions to the more sophisticated. But first of all, let us consider those basic questions.

Why set up an information service?

Everybody has information needs but not everybody is equally capable of satisfying those needs.[1] This is increasingly so in what has been termed our 'information society', with its complexity and rapidly accelerating rate of political, social and economic change. Information is now also seen as a commodity, with a market value that may well put it beyond the reach of the 'have-nots'. More and more, it is being made available in electronic forms which may require the possession of special skills on the part of those wishing to access it. Therefore, a good reason for setting up an information service may well be to make it easier for individuals or groups of people who do not have their own adequate information networks to gain access to information that can be of benefit to them.

Some places or groups that warrant particular attention are the following:

- *inner-city areas* where multiple deprivation exists – bad housing, high unemployment, inadequate schools – or where there is a greater proportion of ethnic minorities and transient populations;
- *housing estates* which lack basic social and other amenities – meeting places, recreational space, shops – where transport is inadequate or expensive, housing is bad, repairs deficient and vandalism rife;
- *rural areas* where facilities – shops, post offices, doctors, clergy, local government services, transport – are fast disappearing;
- *groups with special needs* – low-income families, elderly and disabled people, ethnic minorities, young people, patients, community and social workers.

It is not a good idea to set up an information service because other agencies are doing so and you do not want to be left out. There has to be substantial evidence of need for such a service in the local community or amongst your clientele to justify provision. This leads in turn to the next question.

Who needs an information service?

Rarely will the need for an information service be readily apparent or clearly voiced by your clientele. More often than not, that need will have to be identified and assessed. There are several ways of finding out who needs an information service, ranging from the simple to the sophisticated. Here are a few methods you may care to consider:

2

1 *Talk* to the 'gate-keepers' in your community – these are the people to whom, because of the nature of their work, their knowledge, approachability or status, others go for information and advice. A typical list of 'gate-keepers' might include community workers, trade union stewards, youth leaders, headteachers, Women's Institute secretaries, or GPs. A word of caution: you should not rely on the views of these people alone, as they may well be biased or blinkered. It is important to check out the views of community leaders or 'gate-keepers' against those of your potential clientele and by using some of the other methods below.

2 *Contact* groups and attend meetings. Find out if there are any groups which represent the people you wish to serve, as they will most likely be aware of the needs of their members or of the community. Particularly useful are 'umbrella' groups like Councils for Voluntary Service (CVSs), Rural Community Councils (RCCs), councils for the disabled, trades councils, and community associations. Look out also for less formal groups such as luncheon clubs for community workers, youth leaders or advice workers. Attending meetings of groups like these will give you a feel for the kind of problems that arise and for which provision is lacking. Such meetings might also be a useful forum to discuss the need for any proposed information service.

If your 'community' is a closed one, such as the staff of a particular organization, then it is important for you as information officer or librarian to be thoroughly conversant with the issues of concern to that organization. One way of achieving this more quickly is to have the right to sit in on committee meetings. This will help in identifying what the organization's information needs are likely to be and how to meet them. However, you may need to convince committee members of the desirability of this. One of the best ways is to prove your worth by providing them with some information, possibly on subjects under discussion in the committee.

3 *Arrange an informal meeting* of representatives of groups in your community and other interested or useful people, at which you can discuss your ideas for an information service and then take things further if there is a positive response. Out of this meeting might well be set up a steering committee or working group which could canvass wider opinion, either informally by calling an open meeting, or by conducting a survey of the community. Such a group might also prepare a feasibility study.

4 *Call an open meeting* at which your 'community' can hear about the proposals and make comments. If the meeting is not being called by the kind of steering committee suggested above, in some circumstances it may be helpful for it to be held under the auspices of a neutral body; for example, where your organization, rightly or wrongly, is perceived by the community as representing one particular viewpoint.

Wide publicity for the meeting is essential, using whatever means are available – word of mouth, posters, leaflets, local press, periodicals, newsletters, etc. Try to get the publicity into those areas where large numbers of your 'community' are likely to see it. Any publicity should give details of what the meeting is about, when and where it is being held and at what time it starts.

Choose a date and venue that is convenient to most of the people you want to reach, taking care to avoid other events or activities that are likely to prove a counter-attraction. This may even apply to what is on television at the time! It is wise to give some thought to the ambience of the venue for, in some cases, an imposing room or 'official' building may inhibit attendance or discussion. If at all possible, avoid holding the meeting in a room that is not accessible to disabled people. Refreshments, if only a cup of coffee, help to stimulate a feeling of informality and encourage discussion. Put yourself in the place of someone who might attend the meeting and ask what would attract *you*.

Make careful preparations before the meeting takes place, including a plan of how you would like the meeting to be structured, so that discussion does not waffle on aimlessly and yet is flexible enough to encourage responses from the audience. Graphic displays, audiovisual presentations and speakers from similar projects elsewhere can add another dimension and help to get your proposals across.

Some further tips about the meeting:

● you will need someone, preferably a respected figure in your community, to open the meeting, explain what it is all about, and chair the proceedings;
● keep items as brief as possible – people soon get bored with lengthy speeches;encourage questions and contributions from the floor even to the extent of planting a few 'stooges' to break the ice;

● end the meeting before people get restive or discussion degener-
ates into irrelevancies;

● make it clear what the next step is going to be. If there is support
for your ideas, then you may want to form a committee from those
present. Alternatively, this step may still be premature, in which
case arrange a further meeting of interested parties. Take note of
the names and addresses of those expressing an interest so that
you can keep them informed of future meetings and developments.

So, by the end of the meeting, you should have some measure of
the support for and/or interest in your proposed information service
from the community. It is important that the community or users of
the proposed service are given an opportunity to participate in both
its planning and running, so that it matches their needs and is respon-
sive to changing circumstances. If there is no support, it would be
unwise to go ahead, at least in the form that was proposed.

5 *Conduct a survey* of potential users to establish their information needs. This can be done instead of or in addition to holding an
open meeting. It is essential from the start that you have a clear idea
of what you want to learn from the survey and at whom it is aimed,
for this will determine the kind of questions you will want to ask and
the form in which you present them. It is a good principle always to
try to make the wording simple and unambiguous, with alternatives
spelled out where appropriate, as in the example from South Molton
shown here (Figure 1) which was used to establish the need for a
multi-agency information and advice service in a small market town
in Devon.

When Terence Brake set up a community information service at
South Hackney School in London, he rightly surmised that many of
the pupils would not understand or use the term 'information' and
some might even react with hostility to an emotive word like 'need'.
Consequently, he devised a range of simple questionnaires related to
the youngsters' interests, such as the one on use of leisure time
illustrated here (Figure 2) – which elicit the information in a way
which is less formal and with which the young people can identify.

5

```
SOUTH MOLTON LIBRARY: COMMUNITY INFORMATION PROJECT                "20 QUESTIONS"
Please fill in the answers requested, or delete the words which do not apply.  (If you have
already received and completed one of these, please pass it to a friend).

1.   On what subjects have you needed information, advice     ...........................
     or help in the past year?
     Examples: education, housing, tax, holidays.             ...........................
                                                              ...........................

2.   To which organisations or people have you turned for    ...........................
     such help?
     Examples: neighbour, solicitor, councillor,             ...........................
     Citizens' Advice Bureau, Volunteer Bureau               ...........................

3.   How often do you use South Molton Library?              Frequently/occasionally/never
4.   Do you use any other library in the area?    Yes/no      If so which? ..............
5.   How often do you use the mobile library
     service based on South Molton?                           Frequently/occasionally/never
6.   Do you use another mobile or other service? Yes/no       If so which? ..............
     Example: school library. How often?                      Frequently/occasionally/never

7.   Do you have access to a telephone?           Yes/no      If so which?  Own 'phone/
                                                              neighbour's 'phone/public
                                                              call box or payphone
8.   Do you listen to Morning Sou' West (BBC radio)?          Yes/no
9.   Do you have a television?                                Yes/no

10.  Do you normally do your weekly shopping in South Molton? Yes/no
11.  If not, which town do you visit?                        ...........................

12.  Do you drive or have access to a vehicle?               Yes/no
13.  If not, how far are you from the nearest 'bus stop
     served by a weekly or more frequent service to
     South Molton?                                           ...........................

14.  Which local newspapers and magazines do you read?       ...........................
     (Include parish newsletters and magazines)              ...........................

15.  How long have you lived in the South Molton area?       ...........................
16.  If you are not a "native" of the area, where did
     you live before moving here?                            ...........................

17.  How far do you live from the centre of South Molton?    ...........................

18.  Which of the following age groups are you in?   (Male)   0-16☐ 17-39☐ 40-64☐ 65+☐
     (Please put a tick in the appropriate box)    (Female)   0-16☐ 17-39☐ 40-59☐ 60+☐

OPTIONAL QUESTIONS   The following two questions may be left unanswered but if you do choose
                     to answer them, this will be most helpful to us.  Please note that ALL
                     RETURNED QUESTIONNAIRES WILL BE TREATED AS CONFIDENTIAL.
19.  What is your occupation? ........................        Please put a tick here if you
20.  What is your name and address?                          would like to talk to the
     ...............................................         Project Officer about any item
     ...............................................                                    ☐

THANK YOU FOR ANSWERING THESE QUESTIONS - PLEASE RETURN THIS LEAFLET TO THE PERSON WHO GAVE IT
TO YOU OR DROP IT IN AT THE LIBRARY AT 1 EAST STREET, SOUTH MOLTON.
```

Fig. 1 South Molton Community Information Project survey (reproduced by kind permission of Devon Library Service).

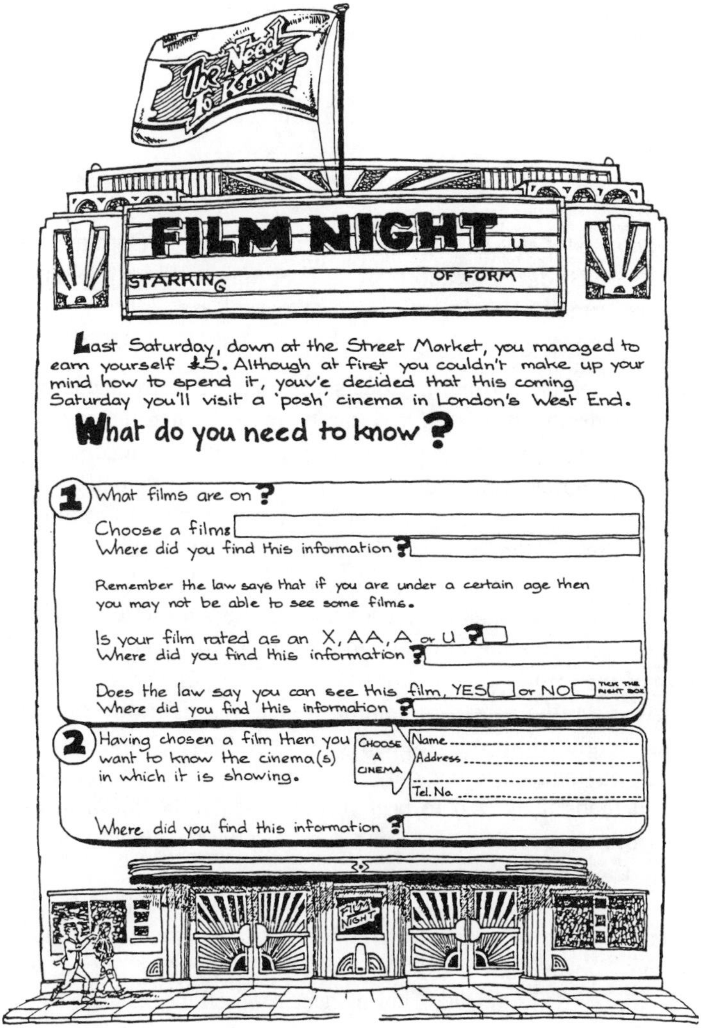

Fig. 2 South Hackney School 'The Need to Know' Project questionnaire (from The need to know: teaching the importance of information. Final report for the period January 1978–March 1979, British Library Research & Development Department, 1980, BLR&DD Report 5511).

The drafting of surveys and questionnaires requires a degree of skill not possible to examine here, but if you would like to know more, the following books should help:

Line, Maurice B., *Library surveys: an introduction to their planning, procedure and presentation,* 2nd edn rev. by S. Stone, Bingley, 1982.

Moore, Nick, *How to do research,* 2nd edn, Library Association, 1987.

The Plain English story, Plain English Campaign, Outram House, Whaley Bridge, Stockport SK12 7LS, £6.40 – most of this book gives practical help on how to write and set out official documents.

The method of distributing your survey questionnaire needs careful attention. Ideally, it helps if you can be present when the respondent fills in the form, so that any points or questions not understood can be clarified. Often valuable information is imparted verbally through hints and nuances of conversation that would not be transmitted on paper. However, the ideal is seldom attainable and you may have to be content with mailing out your questionnaires. This obviously saves time but you should not expect a very high response rate. It helps, of course, where you can afford it, to include a reply-paid envelope for return of the form.

Surveys can be a help in pointing you in the right direction or by adding weight to already formative ideas; however, they should not be used on their own, but only in relation to evidence obtained by other methods. It is well to bear in mind that in the act of setting a framework of questions for your survey, you are already, to some extent, determining the response.

6 *Analyse enquiry statistics* to see if there is a demand from any particular group of user which requires special attention, such as a separate information or advice service. For example, recent years have witnessed the introduction of debt counselling services by Citizens' Advice Bureaux as a response to a vast increase in enquiries in this area. Your organization may already be operating a more traditional reference or information service. An analysis of its enquiries over a period of time, if these are kept in sufficient detail, may indicate areas of need not being adequately met. An alternative, if your statistics are not detailed enough, is to carry out a short-term

monitoring exercise. As well as your own statistics, you might get some help from those of other information and advice agencies operating in your area of interest.

By using some or all of the above methods you should have arrived at an idea of the information needs of your community. However, before making a decision on the kind of service required to meet those needs, it is essential to have as complete a picture of your community as possible. The best way to achieve this is to compile a community profile.

Community profiling

This is a systematic process developed initially by corporate planners and adopted by other agencies, including public librarians, to enable them to plan and provide services which meet the needs of a given community. A typical profile will include:

- *Statistical data* about the population: size, rate of growth, age ranges, sex, marital status, religion, ethnic groups, diseases and mortality, employment, education, housing, etc. Much of this information is obtainable from census documents, supplemented and updated by figures from local authority departments, health authorities, employment centres, police, etc.
- *Socio-economic information:* types of economic activity, community services – statutory, voluntary or private, recreational facilities, meeting places, clubs and societies, etc.
- *Local issues:* redevelopment, unemployment, poor housing, transport problems, racial prejudice, etc.
- *Residents' viewpoints:* letters to the press, community newspapers, local radio and TV, action groups, community noticeboards, graffiti, informal discussions with those who come into contact with a wide cross-section of the community, informal contacts in pubs, shops, public meetings, etc.

The important thing to remember when compiling a community profile is not to rely on one type of information alone as this will give you a biased view. Try to get a fully rounded picture by including both statistical data and subjective assessment, official opinion and residents' reactions, majority and minority viewpoints. Obviously you must tailor your approach to the kind of community you are analysing. Community profiles were initially designed for analysing geographical communities but the same principles will apply, although the techniques and sources of information may vary, if your community is a 'closed' one, such as a school or organization, or a group with special needs, like elderly or disabled people.

There are also some spin-offs from compiling a community profile. If you do decide to go ahead and set up an information service, the information gathered for the profile could form the basis of your local information file and might also be made available to your clientele in printed form. The valuable contacts made with individuals and groups will form the basis for your information network.

This is just a brief indication of what comprises a community profile, if you want more detail, the following may be of help:

Beal, Christina, *Community profiling: a practical manual,* Centre for Research on User Studies, University of Sheffield, 1984.

'Community analysis and libraries', *Library trends,* **24** (3), January 1976.

Jordan, Peter and Whalley, E.D., *Learning about the community: a guide for public librarians,* School of Librarianship, Leeds Polytechnic, 1977.

Library operations checklist No. 3 Compiling a community profile, Public Libraries Group, 1986, £1.75.

Profiling the community: guide for librarians. Vol. 1. Handbook on community profiling; Vol. 2. An analysis of the community served by Southwick Branch Library, Borough of Sunderland, Department of Recreation and Libraries, 1986, £10.00.

The following conclusions, taken from the above issue of *Library trends,* sum up concisely the right way to approach the question of who needs an information service:

1 Formal and informal methods ... are essential both for developing a clear and useful picture of 'who is out there' and for an understanding of what they need/want.

2 There is no substitute for direct, active information-seeking ... in order to avoid acting on unsubstantiated assumptions about groups of people.

3 Just as different communities will want or need different services, different approaches will have to be used ... There is no single approach which will always work, but respect and flexibility are always essential.[2]

Remember also that some information needs may not become apparent until your community information service is up and running and it ought, therefore, to be flexible enough to adapt to them. Determining needs is not a once-and-for-all exercise but a continuous process.

What community information services already exist?
There is one more step that needs to be taken before you can get down to putting flesh on your ideas and that is to find out if there are any other agencies in your area operating identical or similar services to the one that you are planning. You may, in fact, want to take this step at an earlier stage or you might have found out the information in the course of conducting a community profile (see p. 9). Either way, it is an important stage that should not be omitted, since it is in nobody's interest to duplicate existing services, especially if there are gaps in provision elsewhere.

Information about existing services in a particular neighbourhood can be collected by means of a questionnaire (see p. 5 for advice on conducting surveys and questionnaires). This will give you only the bare outlines and will need to be expanded by personal visits.

The kind of information you will need to collect about each agency consists of the following:

- location, premises and equipment, opening hours, how to contact the agency;
- staffing, information resources, training;
- the agency's activities;
- referrals, relationship with other agencies;
- the agency's users;
- feedback to policy-makers;
- publicity;
- management and funding.

This list was taken from *Who knows?: guidelines for a review of local advice and information services, and how to publicise them* (National Consumer Council, 1982) which is an excellent guide to conducting such reviews and provides more details under each of the headings. See also the following:

Going for advice (2 vols.), London Advice Services Alliance, 1987, £8.75 – a manual for conducting reviews of advice services and preparing local development plans.

If it is local agencies that you want to identify and you are not a public library, then try your local library for a start. Other sources might include the Citizens' Advice Bureau, Council for Voluntary Service, Rural Community Council, Social Services Department, civic information bureau and individuals, e.g. community workers, social workers. For groups serving special needs, try organizations like Age Concern, DIAL (Disablement Information & Advice Line), Council for the Disabled, MIND (for mental handicap), or associations of youth clubs.

There are also some national directories of information and advice services which may list or give a lead to local groups:

Consumer Congress directory, Consumer Congress, c/o National Consumer Council, annual – lists organizations in the consumer movement, including advice centres.

Counselling & psychotherapy resources directory, British Association for Counselling, 1991.

Directory of educational guidance services., Advisory Council for Adult and Continuing Education (ACACE), 1982.

Directory of independent advice services, Federation of Independent Advice Centres (FIAC, 1990).

Directory of Welsh consumer organisations Welsh Consumer Council, 1990.

Disability rights handbook. Disability Alliance ERA, annual – lists national information and advice services and local DIAL centres and other local disablement advice centres.

Tourist information centres in Britain, English Tourist Board, annual.

Youth access referral directory, Youth Access, 1992.

Having gone through the above process, you should now have a clearer picture of which community information services already exist in your community or area of interest and where there are any gaps in provision. You should also have some idea of the strengths and weaknesses of existing services and thus be in a position to make a decision about your own proposed service. At this point there are several choices open to you:

1 *Maintain and strengthen the existing provision*. It may be that your community is adequately covered by information services, in which case your efforts might best be channelled towards helping to strengthen and maintain those services. The costs of providing an

information service rise continually and funding for many organizations is frequently precarious. Material support or behind-the-scenes lobbying to help existing services will usually be more than welcome.

2 *Extend an existing service.* The solution to meeting the information needs of your community does not necessarily have to be your direct responsibility. It may not be appropriate, anyway, if your staff do not have the training, flexibility, time or independence to provide the kind of service that is required. There may well be an existing information and advice service which is prevented from providing an adequate service or extending its work through badly located premises or lack of funds for staffing, training, information resources, etc. Your organization could make an appreciable difference by:

● offering free use of suitable accommodation to relocate the service in a place more accessible for the public;
● offering similar accommodation for the location of extension services;
● offering the use of mobile service points, where feasible, so that remote areas of the community can be reached;
● providing help with staffing or resources, e.g. you may have staff who can offer a particular expertise on a surgery basis or you might be prepared to supply loan collections of more expensive reference materials;
● providing access points for the public in unserved areas on behalf of the information service, e.g. by having available postal enquiry forms or providing a direct-line telephone link to the service's central office.

3 *Cooperate.* Although your analysis may show that there are gaps or shortcomings in existing provision, that should not be a signal to leap in immediately and set up a new service. At a time of financial stringency, it makes sense to explore first of all the possibilities for cooperation and thus to get a more rational and coordinated use of resources. This could take the form of one or more of the following suggestions:

● *Sharing information.* Public libraries, for example, could explore ways of putting their extensive information resources, both materials and staff, at the service of other information and advice agencies by agreeing to keep and update files of local information or by producing a directory of local information and advice services.

- *Joint collection, processing and dissemination of information.* Often several agencies in a community will be collecting local information. This is wasted effort, as the information needs to be collected only once, and causes annoyance to those supplying the information. A joint approach is called for, either one organization collecting the information on behalf of the others, or a consortium of organizations sharing the task.
- *Shared premises.* There are distinct advantages in several agencies sharing premises, in addition to that of economy. It provides better access for the public who can see a number of agencies in one place without a time-consuming and often expensive run-around. Referral is made easier, which is particularly useful in multi-problem cases. There is the possibility of not only shared accommodation but also shared information resources, shared publicity, shared case-notes, etc. Sharing can make the service available for longer hours than one agency on its own could possibly attain.
- *Support groups.* Cooperation of the kind listed in this section can be fostered by the formation of an 'umbrella' group which brings together all the community information agencies in a particular community or area of interest. Such a group could take on activities such as information sharing, joint collection of information, cooperative approach to funding, shared publicity, training and generally creating a greater awareness and understanding of each other's work. Sometimes a number of agencies in an area, who are heavily involved in handling problems of a particular kind and do not have the resources or time to cope adequately with them, can benefit from the creation of a specialist support group to provide training, research, practical assistance (e.g. tribunal work), information materials, current awareness services, or expertise in certain areas, such as law, debt counselling, housing, planning, tax, etc. Many public libraries have been involved in setting up and running 'umbrella' groups. The following references will give you more information about the work of such groups:

Bunch, Allan and Hemmings, Richard. 'Umbrella groups', *Community librarian*, December 1988, 4–5.
Holman, Kay, 'Holding the umbrella', *Public library journal*, **3** (6), 1988, 121–3.

4 *Go it alone.* In the next chapter we shall be looking at the practicalities of setting up an information service if, after careful consideration, you decide to go it alone.

Further reading

Doyle, Matt and Mocroft, Ian, *Working it out: some guidelines for project organisers*, The Volunteer Centre UK, £1.50 – concise, down-to-earth advice for organisers of volunteer projects, including planning; premises and capital; methods of work; and management and support.

References

1 Ward, John, 'Equality of information', *Municipal journal*, **82** (20), 17 May 1974, 595.
2 Croneberger, Robert and Luck, Carolyn, 'Community human information needs', *Library trends*, **24** (3), January 1976, 524.

Chapter Two

Setting up the service

You have now reached the stage where you have:

● made a thorough investigation of the information needs of your community;
● identified where gaps exist in information provision;
● decided on priorities;
● consulted with other agencies and individuals; and
● explored the possibilities of cooperation.

As a result, you have decided to set up your own service. The next step then is to consider what type of service to provide and what will be needed to set it up.

What kind of community information service?
There are a number of functions which can be performed by a community information service, of which the following are the main ones:

1 *Self-help*, as the name suggests, requires that users find the answers to their own problems. The community information service input is directed towards selecting appropriate materials, reprocessing information in a form that can be readily understood, packaging information, and arranging all these materials in a way that is easier for the customer to use. This kind of service is most suitable where there is insufficient staff or lack of trained staff to operate a personal enquiry service, such as a small branch or mobile library, or for deposit in an unmanned centre. It is usual for materials to be assembled, produced or packaged by a district or central office.

2 *Support* for other information services or for groups of professional workers, etc. Where there are adequate information services

for the public, the greater need may be for an information service to support the work of other agencies and workers in the field. This could take one or several of the following forms:

- selective dissemination of information (SDI) which, in essence, involves channelling information to meet the expressed subject interests of groups or individuals (see p. 92 for a more detailed discussion of SDI);
- current awareness services;
- press cuttings service;
- provision of loan collections of reference books;
- provision of publicity and educational materials;
- provision of local information.

3 *Information giving*, which can range from simple directional information to the complex, such as eligibility for housing benefit, and may involve *steering* an enquirer to an agency from whom further help or advice can be obtained, without the service making contact with that source of help or advice.

4 *Referral*, on the other hand, is a more active form of steering in which contact or an appointment is made for the enquirer with an agency who can help. In some cases, it may be necessary to *escort* the client to the agency if it is felt that they do not have sufficient confidence to make contact, may be intimidated by officials, or are likely to have difficulties in explaining their case.

5 *Advice* is information tailored to individual need. Giving advice can be a fairly neutral activity, such as setting out options from which the enquirer must make his or her choice, or it can involve evaluation of options with recommendations as to the best course of action.

6 *Practical help* with writing letters, form filling or making telephone calls.

7 *Advocacy* is needed where a client is not capable of obtaining the information, services, benefits or justice to which he or she is entitled. A positive identification is made with the client's case, which is then argued in front of officials, tribunals or courts on the client's behalf.

8 *Community education*, in the context of information and advice work, is a process of increasing the self-sufficiency of individuals or groups to manage their own affairs, obtain their rights, etc. or to improve their awareness and understanding of issues that affect them.

9 *Community action* involves the information service in playing an active role in precipitating change either by acting itself or by alerting other individuals and groups to campaign. Such action can arise out of an analysis of enquiries received, where it becomes apparent that there is a lack of a service or facility in the community or where a situation exists that is causing injustice or disadvantage to people.

10 *Outreach* is a means of providing information or a service to a clientele wider than that usually served by the community information service, in either geographical or sociological terms. It covers the use of extension bureaux, mobiles and deposit collections as well as the use of media, e.g. newspaper or magazine articles, radio, television, advertising or viewdata.

11 *Counselling* requires a greater commitment of time and level of training to help individuals with problems. At one extreme it can involve simply lending a sympathetic ear to clients who, in externalizing their problems, may thus be better able to face them and arrive at a solution. On the other hand, counselling can lead on to diagnosis and analysis, with ultimate referral of clients to clinics for treatment. Counselling should not be undertaken without specialized training.

Not all these activities will be appropriate to your organization or the community it is intended to serve. Some organizations, for example, have to be impartial, and therefore are precluded from activities which might be construed as 'political' or partisan or from taking sides in a dispute.

Although for the purposes of this book the different functions of an information service have been treated separately, in practice such clear distinctions can rarely be made. The process of information–advice–advocacy is often referred to as a 'continuum'. Boundaries are blurred and not generally recognized by users, even though, in setting up a service, limits have to be placed on its actions. Someone seeking information or help with a problem is not really interested in the philosophy of your organization but in obtaining a satisfactory answer or solution, irrespective of the means used to obtain it. Consequently, some people have argued that it is wrong to set up an information service and attempt to limit its functions to just giving information or advice but not advocacy, since users' expectations may be raised but not completely satisfied. On the other hand, it can be argued that something is better than nothing. The decision must be yours but, in setting up a service, you must have a clear idea of what you expect it to achieve and, if it is necessary to set limits, how to deal satisfactorily with cases that need to be taken beyond those limits.

Structure

The next decision to be made concerns the structure of your service. Is it going to operate from one central point or from a number of outlets? From a static centre or a mobile unit? Obviously, the decision will depend to a great extent on the nature of your community. If it is a rural one, with small, scattered pockets of population, then you may want to consider either using a mobile service point or operating through a network of individuals, e.g. village contacts. If your community is a 'closed' one, such as a school or an organization, then one static centre is likely to be more appropriate. The structure of an information service whose community covers a large geographical area – nation-wide for instance – may need to reflect a greater usage by telephone or post, rather than face-to-face contact with clientele. A general rule, already mentioned but worth repeating, is to start modestly and then expand from a secure base, rather than to overcommit at the start and then have to retract.

Management

An information service is set up to meet the needs of a given community and one of the best ways to ensure that the service meets its objectives is for the community to be represented on its management. A fairly common pattern is for a management committee to be made up of representatives from statutory bodies, the service itself, and from individuals and groups in the community. No one group should dominate the management committee and its chairperson should preferably be neutral. An independent committee is particularly necessary where an information service works in the voluntary sector but receives most of its funding from a statutory body. This is in order to guarantee that undue pressure may not be exerted by the funding bodies on the way the service operates. It may be more difficult for a community information service belonging to a statutory organization to have an independent management committee and, in those circumstances, an alternative would be to set up some form of advisory group representing users.

The responsibilities of a management committee or advisory group might include some or all of the following:

- laying down rules for the use of the service (Figure 3);
- monitoring use and recommending changes;
- suggesting new strategies or areas of work;
- ironing-out trouble spots;
- taking community action where lack of provision or malpractice is identified by the information service;
- lobbying for funds or improved facilities;
- giving specialist advice and help on such matters as budgeting, publicity, law, etc.

Lambeth Information Network

**RULES FOR THE
EXCHANGE OF INFORMATION
AND MATERIAL**

Members undertake so far as possible to make the contents of their libraries, other than confidential material, available to each other and to give assistance in the provision of information.

Members shall be at liberty to decline to supply information or to lend material and further, to limit the period of loan or to restrict its use to consultation on the premises of the member holding the required item.

The anonymity of enquirers will be preserved if requested.

Members shall nominate up to three persons to be responsible for loans and to act as signatories. Requests from persons other than those included in the official List of Authorities for Loans shall not be accepted without formal notification. Member's authorised signatories shall be responsible for ensuring that the rules of the lending organisation are complied with.

Material lent under LINK arrangements shall be returned to the lender on demand or within such period as the lender may specify. Any member failing to comply with this rule may without prejudice to any rights of the lender have his membership of LINK determined.

Members without librarians or information officers shall normally direct their requests to the headquarters of LINK or through the local branch of Lambeth Public Libraries.

Fig. 3 Lambeth Public Libraries 'Link' service rules.

What is needed to start an information service?
Establishing and operating a community information service requires certain resources:

- *finance*: capital and revenue;
- *facilities*: premises and equipment;
- *staff*: paid/voluntary, training, health and safety, etc. (see Chapter Three);
- *a system*: for the collection, processing, storage, retrieval and dissemination of information (Chapter Four).

Financial resources
Whether you are setting up a community information service from scratch or simply adding another function to an existing service, there are bound to be financial implications. Capital expenditure will most probably be required to provide premises, furniture and equipment. Revenue will be required to pay for such considerations as:

- staff salaries and travelling expenses;
- rent and rates;
- heating, lighting, water and telephones;
- insurances;
- stationery;
- publicity and promotion.

This is by no means a comprehensive list but it is essential that a budget or business plan is drawn up, setting out as accurately as possible the costs involved, so that expenses and sources of finance can be identified.

A non-statutory organization setting up an information service for the first time has a number of possible sources of funding:

1 *Local authorities*. Counties, district councils, parish councils are all empowered to make grants for this purpose. They will be the most likely source of substantial continuous funding and the most problematical. Local authority funding is usually given in the form of a grant which usually has to be applied for and agreed each year. Often the decision is made close to the end of the financial year and so an information service may find itself always existing on a financial knife-edge. Changes in the political control of a council can often spark off a reappraisal of support for services. Moreover, there is sometimes covert pressure by local authorities to influence the poli-

cies of organizations they fund, particularly those policies of which the authority disapproves.

Local authorities can also give grants for capital expenditure – premises, furniture and equipment. Some will use their lotteries fund for this kind of grant, but not for revenue funding. In recent years, the introduction of rate-capping and standard spending assessments (SSAs) has severely curtailed the amount of money that local authorities are able to commit to the support of non-statutory services. At the same time, other government legislation on, for example, compulsory competitive tendering is aimed at forcing local authorities to divest themselves of services that can, in the government's view, be better provided by the private or voluntary sectors. This may include local authority-run information and advice services. Where services are operated or taken over by voluntary organizations, there is a growing practice amongst local authorities to set down what is expected of the voluntary organization in a contract which is signed by both parties and monitored. This development has spawned a growing literature, of which the following represent some of the more useful titles:

Callaghan, John, *Costing for contracts: a practical guide for voluntary organisations*, Directory of Social Change, 1992, £8.95.

Edwards, Ken, *Contracts in practice*, Directory of Social Change, 1992, £8.95.

Hawley, Keith, *From grants to contracts: a practical guide for voluntary organisations*, Directory of Social Change, 1992, £8.95.

Woolf, Jo, *The beginner's guide to contracts*, London Voluntary Service Council, 1992, £7.95.

If you cannot get funding from the local authority, it may be prepared to give support in kind, such as the provision of premises (short-term accommodation) or shared accommodation in one of its own buildings, e.g. the library, or community centre. The most likely local authority departments to approach are social services, leisure and amenities, libraries or education. Look out too for officers with titles like 'Community Development Officer', 'Youth and Community Officer', or 'Community Services Librarian', who may be able to advise you on what kinds of financial or other help are available. Your local Council for Voluntary Service (CVS) or Rural Community Council (RCC) may be able to advise you on the right approach to local authorities.

In the London area responsibility for grant-aiding voluntary organizations has been vested in a separate body known as the London Boroughs Grants Scheme. They can be contacted at 5th Floor, Regal House, London Road, Twickenham TW1 3QS (Tel. 081-891 5021).

2 *Government departments and agencies.* There is no doubt that the voluntary sector's prospects of funding from central government are not rosy at this present time, particularly for new projects. Funds available are contracting and many of the government departments are now channelling their grants through other agencies, such as Training and Enterprise Councils (see below). It would be advisable to consult your local Council for Voluntary Service or any of the books listed at the end of this section for the latest position regarding grants. The following sources currently available may be of particular interest for a voluntary organization wishing to set up an information or advice service.

The Public Library Development Incentive Scheme (PLDIS) funded by the Department of National Heritage and administered by the British Library Research & Development Department is also available to voluntary organizations. See below (p. 26) for details of this Scheme.

Training and Enterprise Councils (TECs) are an important local source of funding, much of it coming from the Department for Employment. They will be particularly interested in projects that stimulate local employment, provide help for the unemployed, or offer educational guidance. From 1992/3, TECs are administering an Ethnic Minority Grant which forms part of Section 11 funds but projects will almost certainly need to involve training, employment and/or enterprise. Unlike local government bids for Section 11 funding which can only cover revenue costs, TECs will be able to cover project costs.

Rural Development Commission is concerned to alleviate economic and social problems in rural England. Its Rural Social Partnership Fund supports voluntary organizations in partnership with other agencies which aim to tackle problems of rural disadvantage. This fund was set up for three years, starting in 1989, so you will need to contact them to see if it is continuing.

The following books may help you tap central government resources:

The central government grants guide, new edn, Directory of Social Change, 1992, £12.95.

Jones, M., *Government grants: a handbook for non-statutory organisations*, 6th edn, Bedford Square Press, 1991, £6.95 – also covers European Community and local authority grants.

3 *Local and national trusts* are increasingly a useful source of funding for capital expenditure items but are less likely to provide revenue funding, except for innovative or experimental projects. Charities and trusts often have rules concerning what kind of project they can support. It is useful if you can find out what these are before applying since a little redrafting of your proposal could make it more acceptable. District Councils are supposed to keep a list of local charitable trusts and their terms of reference, but failing that the local CVS or RCC will usually be able to advise on possible sources of local funding. National trusts and their areas of interest are listed in *The directory of grant-making trusts*, an annual publication from the Charities Aid Foundation. You should find a copy in the reference section of most major public libraries. A similar type of trust administration that has appeared in recent years is the 'community trust'. Community trusts are independent bodies who receive money from a variety of sources – trusts, industry, local government – and give grants to voluntary projects. Applications may have to be siphoned first through the local CVS or RCC.

Some helpful advice on raising money from trusts can be found in:

A guide to the major trusts, 1993/4 edn, Directory of Social Change, 1992, £14.95.

Norton, Michael, *Raising money from trusts*, 2nd edn, Directory of Social Change, 1989, £7.95.

Directory of Social Change also publishes a magazine, *Trust monitor*, which contains information on new trusts, changes in policies, facts and figures, feature articles, etc.; three issues a year, subscription £20.00.

4 *Commercial organizations* are unlikely to provide funding for the day-to-day running costs of an information service but may be a useful source of capital funding for equipment, furniture or special projects. They may also give help in kind – donations of redundant

equipment, training, etc. – or offer sponsorship deals for fundraising events and publicity.

More details of the kind of help available from the commercial sector will be found in:

A guide to company giving, 1993/4 edn, Directory of Social Change, 1992, £14.95.

Humble, Stephen, *High Street giving*, Directory of Social Change, 1990, £7.95.

The major companies guide, 2nd edn, Directory of Social Change, 1991, £14.95.

Norton, Michael, *Raising money from industry*, 2nd edn, Directory of Social Change, 1989, £5.95.

Directory of Social Change also publishes a quarterly magazine, *Corporate citizen*, which gives up-to-date facts and help with understanding the corporate viewpoint; this costs £30.00 a year for voluntary organizations, £55.00 for others.

5 *European Community* in certain circumstances makes grants to local authorities and to voluntary organizations for schemes which seek to alleviate deprivation or inequality. The European Social Fund is open to organizations that arrange training aimed at providing the skills needed for specific kinds of jobs. Applicants need to have agreement from central or local government to fund at least half (35% in Northern Ireland) of the costs of the training. The allocation of ESF grants has been decentralized and, as far as the voluntary sector is concerned, applications are handled and placed in priority order by the National Council for Voluntary Organizations. Final decisions are taken by the Department of the Environment.

The European Community also administers many small schemes for making grants. These small schemes very rarely have more than a few thousand pounds available for any one project and rarely make more than one grant for the same activity. Grants must also be used in the year they are made. They are thus not much use for core funding but may contribute to set-up costs. Areas covered by schemes include employment, families, older people, disabled people, human rights education, women and combating racism and xenophobia.

More details of what is available from the European Community will be found in:

Davison, Ann and Seary, Bill, *Grants from Europe: how to get money and influence policy*, Bedford Square Press, 1991, £7.95.

There are numerous guides to obtaining grants and fundraising which cover all the sources of funding listed above and many others. Some of these guides are general in extent, others cover particular areas of concern or geographical areas. Here are a few you might like to consider:

Clarke, Sam, *The complete fundraising handbook*, Directory of Social Change/Institute of Charity Fundraising Managers, 1992, £9.95.

Environmental grants, new edn, Directory of Social Change, 1993.

HIV & AIDS: a funding guide for England and Wales, Directory of Social Change/Terence Higgins Trust/National AIDS Manual Publications, 1993, £7.95.

The London grants guide, 2nd edn, Directory of Social Change, 1992, £12.50.

Norton, Michael, *How to write better fundraising applications*, Directory of Social Change, 1992, £9.95.

The West Midlands grants guide, Directory of Social Change, 1991, £9.95.

Directory of Social Change also produces a set of 8- and 12-page *Fundraising* leaflets on *Setting up*; *Planning a capital project*; *Drawing up a budget*; *Raising money locally*; *Earning money*; *Organising an appeal*; *Doing research*; *Writing an application*; *Social sponsorship*; *Developing a strategy*; *Organising an event*; *Fundraising sources*. A complete set of 12 leaflets costs £7.50 or they can be bought separately at 75p each.

If a statutory organization, such as a library, wants to set up a community information service then, in addition to whatever funding can be provided from within its own budget, the following are the most likely sources of funding:

1 *The Public Library Development Scheme (PLDIS)* was set up in 1988 to encourage new enterprises designed to extend or improve public library services in England. Activities likely to promote cooperation between public libraries and other libraries or organizations in the public or private sector are of particular interest. The Scheme is funded by the Department of National Heritage and administered by the British Library Research & Development Department. It was

originally funded for three years, but in September 1990 the Minister for the Arts set aside up to £250,000 per year for the three financial years 1992/3–1994/5. The Scheme provides up to 40% of the funding for projects, the remainder to be found by the library authority or other organization and its partners. Applications can be made by such as the following:

- English local library authorities or their co-operative agencies, such as regional library bureaux;
- any public or private organization (including those in the voluntary sector) able to demonstrate that the proposed development will contribute to the quality and cost-effectiveness of public library services in England or in a particular region; applicants are normally expected to involve one or more public libraries in the project.

Types of project in the community information field that have been helped through this Scheme include a feasibility study and implementation of a Training Shop in Peterborough Central Library, and Camden's Free Leaflets Information Service.

At the time of writing, it is not known whether PLDIS funding will be available for a further three years. Details may be obtained from Christine Burden, Public Library Development Incentive Scheme, The British Library Research & Development Department, 2 Sheraton Street, London W1V 4BH (Tel. 071-323 7042).

2 *The British Library Research & Development Department* has given support over the years to innovative community information services such as South Hackney School 'Right to Know' project and South Molton Community Information project. If your proposed information service intends to break new ground then you may be able to interest the British Library (BL) in a research proposal. It would, however, need to cover the research element of the work. Only in exceptional circumstances has the BL provided financial help towards the setting-up and running costs of projects. The Department has a five-year plan for priorities in research of which the broad areas of concern are the applications and implications of information technology, information as a tradable commodity, and the effects of economic and social constraints on services. Further details of current priorities are contained in their booklet, *Priorities for research 1989–1994*, available from The British Library Research & Develop-

ment Department, 2 Sheraton Street, London W1V 4BH (Tel. 071-323 7060).

Although most of the possible sources of funding listed above are for either capital items or relatively short-term running costs and do not solve the question of how to keep the service going in the long term, nevertheless they do make it possible to get services off the ground, to establish them on a sound footing and to demonstrate their worth to the community. Hopefully, this will then attract more secure and lasting financial support.

Many services provided by local authorities are encouraged to pursue income generation as a means of supplementing or making up a shortfall in budgets. There does not appear to be much scope in the field of community information for income-generation activities, other than marginal activities such as the sale of mailing lists to commercial organizations (a dubious practice at best). The one exception is in the provision of support activities, such as Camden's Free Leaflet Information Service, which is attracting support from libraries and other organizations nation-wide through a subscription system. Other organizations like the National Association of Citizens' Advice Bureaux successfully market their information service but this does not represent a major proportion of their funding.

A community information service that is intended to be simply an extension of an existing statutory service will still need to be costed and the effect on other parts of the service assessed. It is highly unlikely that there will be spare capacity – either finance, staff or accommodation – lying around waiting to be used. A sufficiently well thought out and argued scheme might attract additional funding from the authority or via other sources of finance, but the most likely scenario is that it will have to be provided out of the existing budget. This then means that some kind of re-assessment of current services must take place, in order that priority be given to the proposed service, and resources diverted to support it. It hardly needs to be said that for such a process to take place and be successful, both senior management and staff in the workplace need to be convinced of the value of the new service and to be committed to its development.

The climate for developing such services in public libraries in the mid-1990s is not of the best. Government legislation has focused attention on the 'core' services – lending books and providing reference and study facilities – and other services are expected to be self-financing. Pressure on local authority budgets as a result of rate-capping or the threat of it has meant a retraction of staff involved in outreach services, such as community information. Nevertheless, public libraries are still managing to come forward with innovative schemes, but the watchwords now are 'partnership' and 'income generation'.

Facilities

Location
The choice of a suitable location for your information service will depend to a certain extent on what can be afforded and on the community you will be serving. If you already have suitable premises with spare capacity which can be used, this will help keep costs to a minimum but, if not, you will need to look elsewhere. It is always a good principle to try to locate an information service where it will be most accessible for its users. Even in a 'closed' community, such as a school or organization, there may be parts of the building that are natural congregating points, e.g. hall, refectory, social/recreational rooms, by the drinks machine. Obviously, the location of an information service which does not deal face-to-face with clients, but mainly via the telephone and post, is less crucial. Research into the use of advice centres indicates that most people use them because they are familiar and very local. They also tend to use those which are near their homes in preference to those which are near their workplaces. So the ideal location for an information centre that is to serve the public is likely to be in the neighbourhood shopping area. This will not only make it accessible for the purposive user but should also encourage casual use, especially if it has windows that can be used to promote the service. Such locations, however, can rarely be afforded by one agency alone and you might need to consider sharing with other agencies. Currently, with the recession at its height, there are vast numbers of shop premises lying empty which landlords might consider letting on a short-term basis for a reduced rent. Sometimes district councils have empty property available for short-term lets. And short terms have a habit of being extended...

If obtaining your own prominently sited premises, either alone or shared, is out of the question, then consider the possibility of being housed by another organization that already has premises in a suitable location, such as a library, community centre, council offices, nearly-new shop or even a commercial concern. Failing that, then the next best thing is to seek for premises where there is a significant traffic flow, even though it may not be with shops – for example near a popular bus stop, a school or clinic, on the way to a shopping centre, or in premises which regularly attract a large number of people, e.g. a community centre, library, health or day centre.

An information service that is intended to help those with special needs, such as people with disabilities or elderly people, might be best located in a place where they already meet for other purposes – a day centre or workshop for the handicapped, for example.

The following are some other features to look out for in locating a community information service:

- ground-floor accommodation for ease of access, especially for elderly and disabled people;
- prominent location – not tucked away in a back room or having rear access;
- facilities for display, such as a large picture-window;
- informal atmosphere – some buildings can look too official or have unpleasant associations which may constitute a deterrent to users;
- drop-in facility so that potential users, especially the more timid, have a legitimate reason for going into the centre for the first time to 'suss it out' without being challenged (Figure 4).

Space

The space requirements for your community information service will depend very much on the type of activities it will be undertaking (see pp. 16–19). A *self-help service* makes little demand on office accommodation and does not require an enquiry desk, but will need a prominent location near the major traffic flow in the building and space for noticeboards and leaflet/display racks. A *support service* or one that does not deal face-to-face with clientele may only need an office in any habitable location with space for processing materials. A purely *information-giving service* dealing face-to-face with the public may need a waiting/browsing area that is welcoming and relaxing, space for leaflet display and noticeboards, an enquiry desk

Fig. 4 Drop-in Information Centre, Werrington District Library, Peterborough.

prominently sited near to major traffic flow, and an office/workroom for the staff. An *advice/counselling service*, in addition to the above, will need an interview room(s) for those clients who need privacy. Some advice services put more emphasis on informality and seek collective solutions to problems through group discussion, rather than through a one-to-one approach. Here, the centre becomes more a social facility, encouraging people to drop in for a cup of tea or coffee and a chat, out of which information needs can arise incidentally. This style of operation calls for a kitchen or, at least, space where drinks can be made, and a comfortable lounge-type area. An interview room may still be necessary for those clients who prefer privacy.

Furniture and equipment
Desks, tables and chairs. The importance of the enquiry desk being located near the main traffic flow has already been stated. It should be immediately visible on entering the building/room and clearly signed. Where the location is unfavourable, this can be overcome to some extent by good directional signs. The desk should be low and form the least possible barrier between the information seeker and the staff. It will need to have a fairly large surface to accommodate such things as card files and/or computer, telephone, frequently used quick-reference books, etc. Drawers will be needed for pens,

31

stationery, frequently used information files and cash (where the service has items for sale). A chair will be required for the use of staff, preferably one that is adjustable if more than one person is going to use it, and with a swivel where the staff need to turn round frequently to consult shelves or a noticeboard. There should also be a comfortable chair for clients at the enquiry desk and others nearby for those waiting to use the service, with possibly a low coffee table and some magazines for browsing while they wait.

An information service that handles a high volume of very quick enquiries, like a tourist information centre, might find it more convenient to have a higher bar-type counter with enquirers and staff either standing or using barstools.

Telephone. This is likely to be the most important item of equipment for the staff and the public in your information service. Some information services conduct most of their business with clients over the telephone. In such cases, where it is desirable to link a telephone enquirer immediately with another service, this can be achieved by means of a three-way or conference-line facility. The most useful location for the telephone is on the enquiry desk, although further lines or extensions may be required in interview rooms or offices. Opinions differ as to the desirability of having telephones in interview rooms. In some instances, when seeking information or trying to sort out a problem with another organizsation on behalf of a client, it can be helpful to have the client by the phone so that points can be clarified as soon as they arise. On the other hand, there will be occasions when you will want to talk frankly to another organization without the client overhearing; in which case it is better if the telephone is located in a private office. Ideally, both options should be available but if this is not possible, then you will have to decide on the basis of which will cause the least inconvenience.

Where possible, your information service should have its own separate telephone line so that clients can make contact direct without having to go through a switchboard or waiting for lines to become available. If that is not possible, then an extension exclusively for the information service is the next best thing. It is helpful if you can obtain a telephone number that is easily remembered by users.

There are several instances where people living in more remote areas have been provided with free telephone access to a central information service through the installation of a direct line from a public building, e.g. a branch library. This has been used as an alternative to providing an extension bureau or to compensate for the withdrawal of local offices. The main space requirements would be for a soundproof booth or office. A number of information and advice services have made it easier for clients to contact them by operating a Freefone service or using an 0800 number. Some information services, who need to recover the costs of providing information, are using pay lines, whereby the customer pays not only the cost of the call but also a fee for accessing the information. In these cases, the information is usually provided by means of recorded tape(s). Details of free telephone access services and pay lines can be obtained from your local British Telecom office.

You may consider that it is important for your information service to be able to offer help outside its normal opening hours. In this case you will need to install a telephone answering machine, so that at any hour of the day or night when the service is closed, enquirers can leave messages. Some answering machines also enable you to record a message or information which is played back to callers when they ring the service. The kinds of information which might be appropriate to record in this way are contacts for emergency help, hotel vacancies, 'what's-on' events, bus or train times, etc.

British Telecom produce a useful free booklet, *Telephone helplines: guidelines for good practice*, which gives practical advice on setting up and running telephone helplines. Copies are available from your local BT office.

Computer. Now that microcomputers are within the reach of most information services, they are looked on as being a necessity rather than a luxury. However, if the computer is needed solely for the organization of information, then it may only be of value where you have a particularly large database or need to access the information through a variety of search terms. Otherwise a card index system could be cheaper, quicker to consult and more user-friendly. Generally, a computer is needed for a variety of functions, e.g. maintaining client records, keeping statistics, correspondence, accessing online databases, designing publicity, etc. See Chapter Eight for more details of the use of computers in information and advice work.

Card files. If you are not using a computer for storing your information, it is most likely that your information file will be kept on cards, the most popular sizes being 5in × 3in (127mm × 76mm), 6in × 4in (152mm × 102mm) or 8in × 5in (203mm × 127mm). These cards will need to be housed either in drawers in a wooden or metal cabinet or in open boxes/drawers (wooden or cardboard). Open cardboard boxes designed for card filing are fairly cheap and can be found at most office equipment suppliers. If you are really desperate, shoe boxes make a good substitute. Open wooden boxes are much more expensive but anyone with a smattering of carpentry should be able to knock up some from offcuts of wood. They don't need to be very sophisticated or load-bearing. Open boxes are easy to access and, with appropriate guiding, display the information clearly, but they also have some disadvantages: it is not convenient to stack one on top of the other; they are open to dust, drips from coffee cups, discarded chewing-gum and other unmentionable objects; and, if knocked over, the cards spill out and you have the tiresome job of re-filing them.

Card drawers overcome these problems, even if the information is slightly less accessible. Again, you can get cheap drawers made of cardboard or expensive ones in wood but the most common type is the two- and four-drawer metal filing cabinet. Each drawer holds approximately 1,000 cards and, if you need greater capacity now or later, units can be stacked one on top of the other. Some drawers have a rod which holds the cards in place but this can be a nuisance if you need to take cards out frequently for updating or have information on the back of cards. For even greater storage capacity you will need to consider a free-standing metal or wooden cabinet, but these can be expensive items. With more and more public libraries going over to microfiche or computer catalogues, there may well be an opportunity to pick up such a cabinet at a knock-down price. Enquire at your local public library – but don't mention my name!

There are on the market other more sophisticated files which usually have their own specially shaped cards. If you decide to buy one of these, you will need to take account not only of the cost of the equipment but also of the continuing cost of the specialized stationery. The systems described previously use standard sizes, so that it is possible to use scrap cards or print your own with a predetermined grid to save costs. One card unit that does have some useful features is the Rondofile (Figure 5) which, as the name suggests, works on a turntable system, enabling the user to consult a large number of cards from one sitting position. Cards are easily removed for amendment and are available in a variety of colours, so it is possible to introduce

Fig. 5 Avery Myers Rondofile 600.

an elementary colour-coding of information, say by area, subject or type of organization. A Rondofile is compact enough to be housed on the enquiry desk and thus can also be accessible to the public, if desired. One file holds 1,000 cards and, if more capacity is required, a second unit can be stacked on top. For details and up-to-date prices of Rondofiles contact M Myers & Sons Ltd, PO Box 16, Vicarage Street, Langley Green, Oldbury, Warley, West Midlands B68 8HF (Tel. 021-552 3322). The same firm has other card filing systems, including the Rondex, a rotating desktop file that holds up to 1,000 cards, available in three versions to take any of the standard card sizes referred to above.

Fig. 6 Rotadex rotary vertical card file RV A6/500.

A similar card filing system using a vertical rotary action is made by Rotadex Systems Ltd, 3/5 Fortnum Close, Kitts Green, Birmingham B33 0JL (Tel. 021-783 7411). There are 24 models in the range suitable for five different card sizes, the largest housing 9,000 cards (Figure 6).

Many office equipment suppliers have these systems in stock.

Filing cabinets. Filing cabinets and dividers will be needed for keeping flimsy publications such as pamphlets, leaflets, broadsheets, posters, etc. as well as correspondence. Cabinets come in one-, two-, three- or four-drawer units, usually in metal, although there are some cheap cardboard ones on the market. At a pinch you could always make do with cardboard boxes and used manila envelopes!

A range of reasonably cheap storage and filing units for cards and documents is available from Neat Ideas Mail Order, Sandall Stones Road, Kirk Sandall Industrial Estate, Doncaster DN3 1HT, who will supply a catalogue on request.

Bookshelves. Virtually every information service will have some reference books, varying from a mere handful to many hundreds of volumes. Small numbers can be kept on the enquiry desk itself using bookends (any heavy weight or 'posh' commercial ones), a book slope, or one of those lethal coiled-spring contraptions. Slightly more could be housed on a book trolley and sited conveniently near the desk for quick reference. Larger numbers will require some form of book shelving, even if it is only cardboard or wooden cartons laid on their side or planks suspended across house bricks. There are an infinite number of commercially made metal and wooden shelving units, either free-standing or wall mounted. Your local library should be able to help you with addresses of library furniture and equipment suppliers. Their shelving tends to be more substantial and you may find that bookshop type shelving is both adequate, attractive and cheaper. Some of the major furniture retailers, like Habitat or MFI, have cheap shelving available in a range of bright colours.

Sloping shelves may be needed for displaying magazines, leaflets or information packs face outwards. Most modern library shelving systems have facilities to incorporate sloping shelves. Murrell's and Point Eight (see *Leaflet racks* section below) also do sloping shelf units, either free-standing or wall mounted.

Noticeboards. Noticeboards are needed for displaying posters and information sheets for your clientele. Rarely does a community information service have sufficient noticeboard space, so be generous in your estimate where funds allow. Nothing looks worse than seeing a noticeboard with posters all higgledy-piggledy and overlapping. For cheapness, buy a large sheet of pin-board and cut to size to fill empty wall spaces, pillars, doors, etc. Boards do not need too smart a finish since most of the time they will be hidden by posters. A noticeboard standing or hanging in a window of your centre and visible to the public can be used to feature special events, information campaigns, surgeries, or out-of-hours information. Alternatively, consider using a mobile blackboard or external wall-mounted noticeboard for this purpose. External noticeboards are best covered, using vandalproof glass or perspex. There are many commercially produced free-standing noticeboards. For details of some of these see the section *Display boards* below.

Leaflet racks and dispensers. Considering the vast number of leaflets available of all shapes and sizes, the choice of ready-made equipment for displaying them is not wide and what does exist is often expensive. All the more reason for trying to make your own. The following are two cheap suggestions:

1 Cut stiff manila envelopes of the size required to make pockets, glue them in rows on a large piece of card and pin this onto a wall or noticeboard. An alternative material to use for pockets is adjustable book jacketing, which has an added advantage in allowing all the leaflet to be seen through the plastic front.

2 Screw cup hooks into a sheet of blockboard or similar material, attach to a wall, and hang leaflets from the hooks by punching a hole in the top of them. A copy of the cover of each leaflet could be pasted onto the board to act as an *aide memoire* when stocks have all been taken.

Norank Murrell Ltd, Field Road, Mildenhall, Suffolk IP28 7AR (Tel. 0638 71301) do a variety of fairly cheap, white, plastic-coated wire leaflet and pamphlet racks suitable for various locations: table, wall or free-standing. Their most versatile is a free-standing gondola unit with interchangeable sides to take A4, A5 or $^1/_3$A4 size leaflets.

More up-market leaflet dispensers are available from Point Eight Ltd, Shaw Road, Dudley, West Midlands DY2 8TP (Tel. 0384 238282), including the best one I have seen for holding flimsy A4 leaflets or single sheets (Figure 7). Point Eight also do a range of perspex holders for multiple copies of a single leaflet.

If money is no object, then you might be better off with a custom-designed and made leaflet dispenser.

Display boards. Display boards will be needed if you intend to put on free-standing exhibitions or displays. There are innumerable makes available in a variety of price ranges, many offering special features or accessories. It would pay you to look around first and get advice from someone in the know, such as the publicity officer of a local authority, large firm or other public body. Consider such matters as portability and stability – particularly if you are going to use the boards outside the centre or outdoors – and ease of assembly.

If any display boards can be said to be universal, then it must be those of Marler Haley Exposystems Ltd, who do several different systems that are easy to erect, versatile and attractive. They also have a variety of free-standing noticeboards and a range of accessories such as shelves, lights, leaflet dispensers, etc. which go with both display boards and noticeboards. Prices vary according to range.

**Fig. 7 Hannecke A4 leaflet/maga-
zine spinner – supplier: Point
Eight.**

Write to them for details and prices at Exposystems House, Beacons-field Close, Hartfield, Hertfordshire AL10 8XB (Tel. 0707 268155).

Strip indexes. Strip indexes may be used as an alternative to card files or as a way of presenting information for customers to use. They are limited as to the amount of information that can be contained on a strip, although a variety of widths is available. Strips are more awkward to interfile and update but they have the advantage that it is possible to photocopy quite easily the whole file or sections on demand. As personal computers (PCs) become more universally available, it is difficult to see a future for strip indexes. Kalamazoo do a variety of holders and strips but these are a little expensive. Their address is Kalamazoo Business Systems plc, Mill Lane, North-field, Birmingham B31 2RW (Tel. 021-411 2345).

A cheaper line is available from Datex Systems, Brandsby, York YO6 4SJ (Tel. 034 75224) (see Figure 8).

Other furniture and equipment. It is possible to list a great many other items of furniture and equipment that a community information service might need, depending on the nature of the service, the resources available, and the existence or otherwise of back-up secre-tarial help. I will simply note a few items that may be considered: (a) pigeonholes for storing leaflets; (b) bench or flat surface for as-sembling packs or publications; (c) typewriter; (d) photocopier (be very careful about leasing a photocopier – preferably get legal advice

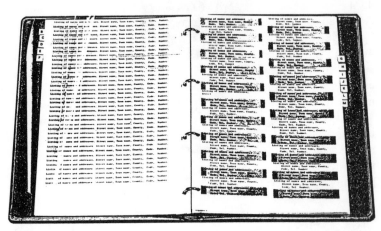

Fig. 8 Datex Slipstrip index.

before signing any contract); (e) machine for recording number of users/enquiries ('clicker'); (f) fax; (g) duplicator – stencil or offset.

Stationery
Pamphlet boxes may be needed for storing booklets, leaflets and other ephemeral materials for use by staff or clientele. They are available in several sizes and varying quality, from cardboard to plastic, closed or open at the top. Lawtons Ltd, 60 Vauxhall Road, Liverpool L69 3AU (Tel. 051-227 1212) do a cheap A4-size cardboard pamphlet box, called the Lawco Box, which comes flat and is then folded into shape. A more up-market A4 fold-up file box in brightly coloured plastic-covered card is produced by Esselte Dymo Ltd, Spur Road, Feltham, Middlesex TW14 0TR (Tel. 081-890 1388). The same firm also has a more rigid (and more expensive) polystyrene plastic pamphlet/magazine file box in bright colours, sizes A4 and A5. Library stationery suppliers also have ranges of pamphlet boxes on offer. Addresses from your local library headquarters.

Manila folders and envelopes to file cuttings, leaflets, information sheets in vertical files. Plastic wallets are even better, if you can afford them, as they enable the contents to be immediately visible. They are particularly useful if you want to go in for compiling information packs for your clients. Celsur Plastics Ltd, Drake Avenue, Gresham Road, Staines, Middlesex TW18 2AW (Tel. 0784 457175–9) have them available in clear and opaque plastic to take A4 documents, and can produce other sizes to your specifications.

Cards: 5in × 3in for subject indexes or brief information, 6in × 4in, and 8in × 5in for recording more detailed information about organizations and services. Cards can be overprinted with a grid for entering information in a standard form. Use scrap cards for cheapness or 'greenness'. Cards are available from most office stationers.

Forms, headed paper, standard letters for collecting information, issuing press releases, correspondence, etc.

Notepads, printed with your logo, opening hours and services, on which to write information for enquirers. These can act as a form of publicity for the service.

Statistics sheets for gathering information about the use made of the service (see pp. 129–34).

Chapter Three

Staffing

Staff are the most important element of a community information service. However efficient and comprehensive the information-gathering system and sophisticated the equipment, if the staff are not – to borrow a piece of computer jargon – 'user friendly' then your service will not attract customers. A bright, helpful and sympathetic person can make up for limited resources, so it pays to concentrate on getting the right one or ones. The right one, in this instance, may not necessarily be the person who is most qualified academically or professionally, as the important characteristics here are a commitment to the aims of the information service and an approachable personality.

It is not possible to lay down any formula regarding the staffing of an information service because there are so many variables. An information service that is merely an extension of an already existing service may be able to make use of the same staff, given that they have sufficient spare capacity, are in sympathy with the aims of the new service and, where necessary, have been adequately trained. Avoid loading extra work on to already hard-pressed staff as this can cause resentment and will not help to ensure the success of the service. Make sure that the administrative and clerical services will be able to cope with any increased demands made by the service (see chart on pp. 44–5). It may be that in order to take on a new function, some aspects of the existing service will have to decline or be dropped altogether. Again, it is important to get staff committed to these changes from the beginning and not to present them as a *fait accompli* without discussion.

If you are starting an information service from scratch, then a decision will have to be made whether it is to be run by full- and/or part-time paid staff or volunteers, or a combination of both. Either way, the first priority will be to obtain a suitable person to organize the service. Such a person will need to have a hand in drawing up job descriptions, selecting staff, recruiting volunteers, arranging training, publicizing the service, setting up the information system and making sure that adequate records are kept. Depending on the type of service, they may also need financial skills. Prepare a job description and a person specification for the post and, if it is to be a paid appointment, set the salary and hours of work (see Appendix 1 for a specimen job description). To find out what salary to offer, check adverts in appropriate periodicals or newspapers for similar posts, approach other information services of a similar type, or contact the umbrella organization, if there is one, for your type of service (see Appendix 2 for a list of addresses). Even where the organizer's post is to be a voluntary one, the degree of commitment expected may warrant a small payment or honorarium. Make it quite clear to whom the organizer is to be responsible.

The number of staff or volunteers you require will depend on the information service you are planning, the opening hours, and the volume of work expected. Opening hours must take account of the needs of your community and of the interests of your staff. Long opening hours obviously make the service more accessible, but the staffing requirement may be too great for the resources available. Staff also like to be kept busy – long periods of inactivity can be demoralizing unless there is 'housekeeping' work that can be done in between enquiries. It is best to aim initially for modest opening hours chosen to suit the likely patterns of most usage and the availability of staff or volunteers. You can always expand or adjust in the light of experience and with further staffing. Research into the use of advice services has shown that there is a sort of threshold of opening hours. Once the threshold is passed, the increase in use is proportionately greater than the increase in hours. If your service is aimed at the public, try to get a mixture – day, evening, lunchtime, Saturday – so that as many people as possible have a chance to visit the service.

The table below (pp. 44–5) sets out some of the main activities undertaken by the staff of each type of information service who are either in direct contact with clientele, working behind the scenes in a supporting role, or providing clerical/secretarial services. In practice, of course, there may not be such a clear division of responsibilities and you may well find all three categories performed by one person.

TYPES OF SERVICE	STAFF FUNCTIONS		
	DIRECT CONTACT WITH INDIVIDUALS AND GROUPS	SUPPORT	CLERICAL
SELF-HELP	(a) Simple directional enquiries and referral (b) Tidying self-help section (c) Maintaining leaflet and poster displays	(a) Identification and selection of appropriate materials (b) Organization of self-help collections (c) Preparation of self-help materials – leaflets, packs, etc. (d) Updating of self-help collections and packs	(a) Typing or word processing of self-help information lists and leaflets (b) Duplicating/printing of same
SUPPORT	(a) Regular contact with groups to identify needs (b) Help with classifying and arranging information files and collections (c) Training in retrieval and organization of information	(a) Selection and assembling of materials for loan collections (b) Scanning of periodicals, etc. for SDI, bulletin, press cuttings services (c) Preparation of same (d) Collecting and organizing local information (e) Preparation of publicity/educational materials	(a) Sending out standard letters (b) Typing of information file entries, bulletins, leaflets, etc. (c) Duplicating/printing of same (d) Inputting to computer database

TYPES OF SERVICE	STAFF FUNCTIONS		
	DIRECT CONTACT WITH INDIVIDUALS AND GROUPS	SUPPORT	CLERICAL
INFORMATION	(a) Information-giving to individuals or groups either face-to-face, by phone or post (b) Maintaining leaflet and poster displays (c) Selling publications, tickets, etc. (d) Booking accommodation	(a) Researching difficult enquiries (b) Collecting, organizing and updating information files (c) Selection of books, pamphlets, etc. (d) Preparation of information guides, packs, etc. (e) Publicity for service – posters, leaflets, radio/TV spots, etc. (f) Preparation of displays	(a) Typing of letters in reply to postal enquiries (b) Typing of information file cards or inputting to computer database (c) Sending standard letters Typing or word processing of information guides etc. (d) Duplication/printing of same
ADVICE, ADVOCACY, COUNSELLING	All activities listed under INFORMATION above, plus: (a) Giving advice on a one-to-one basis (b) Contributing to group discussion of problems (c) Client reception (d) Escort (e) Maintaining case notes (f) Practical help (g) Representation at tribunals, courts, etc.	All activities listed under INFORMATION above, plus: (a) Selection and assembling of materials for loan collections (b) Scanning of periodicals, etc. for SDI, bulletin, press cuttings services (c) Prepation of same (d) Collecting and organizing local information (e) Preparation of publicity/educational materials	All activities listed under INFORMATION above, plus: (a) Typing letters on behalf of clients (b) Typing tribunal case notes

However, the table may be a help in working out the number of staff required.

As well as sufficient staff to cover the hours your service is open, you will also need to make allowances for sickness, holidays, training and unforeseen disasters. So don't rely on just one person: there should always be adequate back-up staff. Most full-time workers in effect only work about 200 days each year, once allowance is made for weekends, holidays and sick leave.

Salaries and service conditions

If your information service is part of a larger organization, such as a library service, then salary scales and conditions of service are likely to have been determined already. Most information and advice workers, even in independent centres, are paid on the Administrative, Professional, Technical and Clerical (APT&C) scales used by local authorities. A job evaluation study in the mid-1980s valued generalist advice centre workers' posts on the following APT&C spinal points and salary scales (figures as at September 1992). I have adjusted the spinal column points to bring them into line with subsequent changes to the APT&C scales.

Post	*Spinal column point*	*Scale*	*Salary*
Organizers and other senior staff	32 and above	SO2 and above	£17,208–
Advice workers working independently	26–31	6–SO1	£14,106–£16,710
Advice workers working with a significant degree of supervision	22–28	5–6	£12,438–£15,063
Clerical and administrative staff	14–21	3–4	£9,930–£12,117

Again, it is fairly common for information and advice workers to be appointed under the National Joint Council (NJC) Conditions of Service which apply to local authority workers. You may hear these conditions of service referred to as the 'Purple Book' from the colour of its cover. The 'Purple Book' covers such matters as holiday entitlement, maternity leave, sickness, travel and subsistence payments etc. Using this book is much simpler than a service having to negotiate all these conditions with its staff.

Many local authorities are now employing staff – particularly senior staff – on a contract basis, usually for three or five years (medium-term contracts). It is a method of employment that may lend itself to those information services whose funding is insecure from one year to the next. Since continuity of employment cannot be guaranteed, staff could be appointed on a short-term contract basis, renewable every year when funding is determined. However, a service would need to weigh up the possible disadvantages that might arise from an insecure workforce, such as low morale. If such a service does decide to offer staff permanent employment, it must be aware of the need to make provision for redundancy in the event of a cut in or withdrawal of funding.

Volunteers

Volunteers can be a great asset in running an information service, provided they are of the right calibre and are suitably trained. Indeed, some services, like Citizens' Advice Bureaux, exist substantially on voluntary help. In recruiting volunteers, you will need to draw up a brief description of the type of work you expect them to do and a personnel specification detailing the qualities you are seeking. You may be overwhelmed with enquiries, since information and advice work is generally regarded as being a very worthwhile and satisfying activity because it is varied, interesting and its effects are often immediately recognizable. Not everyone, however, will be suited to this kind of work, so you will need to take care over selection, particularly if confidentiality is required. The following are some points to look out for:

- What time commitment can the volunteer offer? Is it flexible? Does it meet the hours your service operates?
- Does the volunteer have a personality that is approachable and will encourage clients to seek information or talk about their problems?
- Can the volunteer be trusted to keep confidences to themselves?
- How would the volunteer react under pressure?
- Has the volunteer got initiative and perseverance in seeking information?
- Will the volunteer understand and keep within the rules and regulations of your service?

- Has the volunteer the capacity for training and the ability to recall that training in dealing with clients?
- Has the volunteer the right attitude to accept orders and direction from paid workers or other senior volunteers?

At the same time, paid workers should be sensitive to the needs of volunteers and should make every effort to involve them in the planning and direction of the service. Volunteers give their time and skills free of charge but they should be reimbursed for expenses they incur in doing so. There has been a move in recent years for volunteers, whether employed by a voluntary or a statutory agency, to be issued with a contract in the same way as paid workers.

If you have difficulties in recruiting volunteers on your own, you can get help from your local CVS or RCC. There may even be in your town a Volunteer Bureau which specializes in finding and placing volunteers.

The following books will also be of help:

Adirondack, Sandy, *Just about managing*, 2nd edn, London Voluntary Service Council, 1992, £10.95 – a lively guide to effective management of voluntary organisations.

Darvill, Giles, *The impact of contracts on volunteers*, The Volunteer Centre UK, 1990, £2.00.

Holloway, Christine and Otto, Shirley, *Getting organised: a handbook for non-statutory organisations*, Bedford Square Press, 1988, £5.95.

Step by step: a guide to volunteer fundraising, The Volunteer Centre UK, 1992, £6.00.

Supporting volunteers, The Volunteer Centre UK, 1988, £4.00 – a resource pack providing checklists and notes on good practice, health and safety, insurance, and expenses.

Voluntary but not amateur, 3rd edn, London Voluntary Service Council, 1990, £8.95 – practical guide to the law for new and established voluntary and community groups.

Voluntary work in advice centres: a handbook for workers, centre co-ordinators and management committees, The Sheffield Advice Centres Group, Highfield House, 20 St Barnabas Road, Sheffield S2 4TF, 1989, £5.00 (inc. p&p) – contains some information and addresses of relevance only to the Sheffield area.

Whitcher, Angela, *All expenses paid? The reimbursement of expenses to volunteers*, The Volunteer Centre UK, 1992, £0.50.

Whitcher, Angela, *Making the right choice: guidelines on selecting volunteers*, The Volunteer Centre UK, 1992, £2.50.

Training

Once you have selected your paid staff and/or volunteers, you will need to provide them and subsequent recruits with access to some form of training, depending on the demands of your service. At the very least, it is usual for new staff to undergo an induction programme which should aim to familiarize them with all the aspects of the service – from why it exists to where the light switches are, and the broader context in which it operates. Ideally, you should draw up an induction checklist of all the areas that you need to cover with each new member of staff. If time permits, there is merit in staff spending some time with other information and advice agencies in the area, in order to be aware of the range of services they offer, the type of clientele served and the particular strengths of each organization.

Beyond that, you have to decide whether the skills required to operate the service can be obtained by any of the following:

● formal internal courses;
● informal methods, such as 'sitting next to Nellie';
● external local courses;
● external national courses;
● self-tuitional material.

In addition, you will need to consider for existing staff:

● continuous learning;
● refresher courses.

1 *Formal internal courses.* Organizing your own internal training course has a number of advantages. It can be slanted to the particular needs of the service and the acquisition of basic skills can be practised using the materials and equipment that the recruit will have to hand in operating the service. It can also be combined effectively with practical 'on-the-job' training. Such a course will need to combine formal talks with practical exercises and possibly visits to other information and advice agencies. Usually the presence of 8–10 people is regarded as a minimum for running a formal course. Less than

this and you may want to consider using a combination of continuous 'on-the-job' training and external courses, or combining with one or more agencies to provide a joint training scheme.

Model internal training programmes are set out in the following publications and may be useful in planning your own scheme, bearing in mind that they are based on American community information practice:

Jones, Clara S, (ed.), *Public library information and referral service*, Gaylord Professional Publications, New York, 1978, 98–110.

Turick, Dorothy, *Community information services in libraries* (*Library journal* Special Report no. 5), *Library journal*, New York, 1978, 66–7.

An excellent study on *Education and training for community information and advice work* was submitted by Julia M. Reid as part of her Master's degree at the University of Sheffield Department of Information Studies in 1982. It is not just a theoretical work but contains details of courses that existed at the time, including the reproduction of syllabuses.

2 *Informal training methods.* 'Sitting next to Nellie' is perhaps the most time-honoured method of imparting practical skills and is still one of the most effective, provided 'Nellie' isn't also passing on bad habits. As the name implies, it involves the recruit sitting alongside an experienced information worker or adviser in order to learn how the job is done. Nowadays the technique probably has a more nondescript, non-sexist name, such as 'work shadowing'. It is probably not sufficient on its own to cover all training requirements and will need to be supplemented by other methods.

3 *External local courses.* If formalized training is required and you do not have sufficient new recruits or the resources to warrant running your own course, then look around for any courses already on offer in your area. Some colleges of further education run courses in such subjects as welfare rights, often in conjunction with organizations like Child Poverty Action Group or the Workers Educational Association. Some CVSs or other umbrella groups organize basic training courses or ones on more specialized topics. Some Citizens' Advice Bureaux will open up the National Association of Citizens' Advice Bureaux (NACAB) training scheme to other information and advice workers. Ask at your local bureau or NACAB regional office

for local availability. Training provided by external courses may not exactly match the requirements of your service and will need to be supplemented by some form of internal training.

4 *External national courses.* There is a variety of courses available nationally which provide some training that would be helpful to staff running an information and advice service. These range from academic courses leading to a professional qualification to day courses organized by national information and advice agencies, often specializing in a particular area of work. Space will allow only the briefest of details about the kind of courses available.

● *Librarianship courses.* Most library schools attempt some coverage of community information, if only as part of a more general course, and related skills such as information retrieval. A few library schools feature community information more prominently in both the required and the elective elements of their syllabus. One of the better examples is that of Manchester Polytechnic's Department of Library and Information Studies where all students follow the 'Information Access' course which includes resource-sharing, cooperation, matching needs and services, community profiling, community services, one-stop information shops, evaluation of information services, and monitoring of information needs. In their second and third years, students can also elect to take 'The Local Community' course, the objectives of which are the following:

(a) to develop an awareness and appreciation of the information needs of a variety of localized user communities;
(b) to develop a critical awareness of sources and services available to satisfy those needs;
(c) to gain an understanding of the problems faced by those who are unable to use existing services because of deprivation.

Other library schools offering elective courses on community information include:

University of Sheffield Department of Information Studies
Liverpool Business School Department of Information and Library Studies
University of Northumbria Department of Information and Library Management

University of Central England in Birmingham Faculty of Computing and Information Studies.

University of Wales Department of Information and Library Studies.

The Library Association, 7 Ridgmount Street, London WC1E 7AE (Tel. 071-636 7543) will help with addresses of library schools and advise on library education in general. It also runs a number of short courses on topics, some of which may be relevant to information and advice workers, as does Aslib, 3 Belgravia Square, London SW1X 8PL (Tel. 071-235 5050). Contact them for details.

- *Community work courses* – taught at many colleges of various levels. Most courses have optional subjects that would be relevant to information and advice work, such as welfare rights, housing policy, and law and the community worker. Directories of courses at higher and further education colleges can be found in the reference sections of most large libraries.

- *Voluntary organizations, umbrella groups and other bodies* often arrange short courses for information and advice workers, particularly within their sphere of interest. The most well known is the aforementioned NACAB training scheme, which is usually available on a local or regional basis. Other major providers include:

  - Child Poverty Action Group, 1–5 Bath Street, London EC1V 9PY – runs courses in central, fully accessible locations on such topics as welfare rights, law, lobbying, debt, skills training, etc.
  - National Money Advice Training Unit, Money Advice Services, Birmingham Settlement, 318 Summer Lane, Birmingham B19 3RL (Tel. 021-359 3562) – runs basic courses in debt counselling and county court procedures and a range of specialist courses, including one on 'Self help and telephone advice'.
  - SHAC (The London Housing Aid Centre), 189a Old Brompton Road, London SW6 0AR (Tel. 071-373 7841/7276) – courses on all aspects of housing.
  - Disability Alliance, ERA, Universal House, 88–94 Wentworth Street, London E1 7SA (Tel. 071-247 8776) – courses on all aspects of disability.
  - Federation of Independent Advice Centres (FIAC) – runs

courses on training, various aspects of the welfare benefit system, housing and money advice. Details from FIAC, 4th Floor, Concourse House, Lime Street, Liverpool L1 1NY (Tel. 051-709 7444).

● London Advice Service Alliance (LASA), 2nd Floor, 88–94 Wentworth Street, London E1 7SA (Tel. 071-247 0455) – one- or two-day introductory and in-depth courses held at LASA on all aspects of the benefit system and its applicability to special needs, tribunal work, and taking cases to the commissioners.

● Joint Council for the Welfare of Immigrants (JCWI), 115 Old Street, London EC1V 9JR (Tel. 071-251 8706) – immigration and nationality legislation.

● The Volunteer Centre UK, 29 Lower King's Road, Berkhamsted, Hertfordshs.ire HP4 2AB (Tel. 0442 873311) – a whole range of residential and non-residential courses on various aspects of work with volunteers.

● The Directory of Social Change, Radius Works, Back Lane, London NW3 1HL (Tel. 071-284 4364) – courses on fundraising, accounting and financial management, finance and administration, management skills, communication skills, personal skills, and workshops on the contract culture. Held in London and other major cities.

● National Council for Voluntary Organisations, Regent's Wharf, 8 All Saints Street, London N1 9RL (Tel. 071-713 6161) – courses on a wide range of topics of interest to the voluntary sector.

● *Training packs, videos, etc.* – NACAB has produced a range of reasonably priced self-training packs on using the NACAB information system, income support, undefended divorce, the green form scheme, the 1988 Housing Act, PAYE income tax, unfair dismissal, homelessness, etc. NACAB has also produced some training videos, such as 'Perceptions' – looks at the backgrounds and histories of a number of people coming into a CAB; 'Face to face' – people sit in front of the camera and present a variety of problems; 'Avoiding danger' – health and safety at work; 'Counselling at work'; 'Debt'; 'Industrial tribunal'; and 'AIDS'. Details from NACAB, 115–123 Pentonville Road, London N1 9LZ.

Continuous learning and refresher courses

It is essential that staff of an information service are kept up to date on new information and developments, so you will need to devise a system for ensuring this. One way is to organize a regular staff briefing session at a time when the service is not open to its customers. Sessions can be used not only to impart new information but also to discuss recurrent problems, difficult enquiries and newly-discovered sources of information. It may not be possible to get all the staff together at one time, especially if the service is run by part-time staff and volunteers. In these instances you may need to use a bulletin board or regular staff memos/newsletter.

In addition to continuous learning, your staff may need to attend refresher courses, particularly in subjects they need to know about but do not use regularly, and in order to develop new techniques or keep up to date in ones already acquired.

The following books on aspects of training will provide further help:

Conway, Lisa, *Training*, The Volunteer Centre UK, 1989, £4.50.

Ford, Jane K. and Merriman, Philippa, *The gentle art of listening: counselling skills for volunteers*, Bedford Square Press, 1992, £6.95.

Tackling training, London Voluntary Services Council, 1989, £4.95.

FIAC is planning a companion volume to *Managing to advise*, to be called *Training to advise*, which should be available in 1993. For details and availability contact them at Concourse House, Lime Street, Liverpool L1 1NY (Tel. 051-709 7444).

Health and safety, insurance

Accidents frequently happen in offices, whether by human carelessness or badly positioned or maintained equipment. You will need to train staff to be aware of safety hazards and to set up a system for regularly checking on health and safety matters. Where a service deals face-to-face with the public, there is always the danger of attacks on and harassment of staff. Staff should be trained to defuse conflict situations but you may also need to take other measures, such as not letting staff be alone in the centre with a user and providing panic buttons in private interview rooms.

If your service is going to use visual display units (VDUs), you will need to be aware of new EEC legislation covering safety and use.

Where an information service is not covered by the insurance policies of a parent organization, it will need to make the following provisions in addition to the usual buildings and contents insurance:

- *Employer's liability insurance*, which ensures that the employer is able to meet claims arising from injury, illness or death of an employee where these arise from their work and the employer is legally liable for them.
- *Public liability insurance* is needed to protect you against any claims for injury occurring on the premises and caused by negligence.
- *Professional indemnity insurance* insures against claims by users who have been given incorrect information or advice.

More details of insurance and health and safety will be found in the following books:

- Ford, C. and Silley, A., *Insurance protection: a guide for voluntary organizations,* Bedford Square Press, 1992, £5.00.
- Wasserman, Cressida, *Protecting volunteers*, The Volunteer Centre UK, 1990, £1.00.
- Health and Safety Executive, *Essentials of health and safety at work*, rev. edn, HMSO, 1990, £3.50.
- King, Stephen, *Display screen equipment: a user's guide*, Croner Publications Ltd, 1993, £1.80 (minimum quantity 30).

Chapter Four

The information base

Information is the life-blood of a community information service and the information file is at its heart. Unless the heart is sound and continually pumping a supply of regularly renewed and fresh information into the system, it will not function at its best. Therefore, it is important to give extra care and attention to planning the resources needed to set up a sound information base and a workable system for keeping it up to date.

Some basic things you will need to consider are as follows:

● How is the information to be collected?
● What method is to be used for processing and storing information?
● How is the information to be retrieved?
● What size is the file likely to be?
● What areas, geographical and subject, is the file to cover?

In addition, you will need to consider how the information is going to be disseminated, if it is not just for internal use; but that is the subject of the next chapter.

The kind of system you choose and the degree of its sophistication will depend on the nature of your information service, the size and complexity of the information you need to store, the staff, and the financial resources available. When designing a system, make sure it is readily understandable to all those using it – volunteers and public included – and not just to professionals.

Coverage
In identifying the need for your community information service, you should have reached a decision already on the community to be served. This may be either a geographical community or a community of interest or both. Either way, you will still need to

make a decision about the extent of your information base. For example, a neighbourhood information service must decide what information to collect on the wider area – town, county, region, nation – outside its local community. An information service aimed at a fairly wide area may need to limit its interests to a particular sector of the community or to a particular range of subjects, e.g. the low paid, those receiving income support, or those with debt problems. Even an information service in support of a local campaign may benefit from collecting information on similar campaigns or problems country-wide.

Types of information
The information base of your service is most likely to include the following types of information:

1 *Soft information* – details of clubs, societies, organizations and services; individuals; events, etc. Usually this information will not be available in a published form, or at least not in sufficient detail, and it will be necessary to make a conscious effort to collect it. This information may comprise the major part of the resources file.

2 *Hard information* – factual information on a specific subject e.g. benefit rates for single-parent families, how to get legal aid, how to change your name. This information will be available in a variety of forms, some ephemeral such as leaflets, pamphlets, booklets, broadsheets, posters, periodical articles, etc. Such items are usually kept in a vertical file, in storage boxes or similar receptacles and accessed via some form of index or classification scheme. Other hard information may be in the form of books, multi-volumed reference works, law books, or even audiovisual forms. If there are many items of this type, they will need to be classified and shelved.

3 *Supplementary information* is information already produced in a particular format – directories, handbooks, diaries, annual reports, constitutions, newsletters – of organizations appearing in your information file.

'Soft' information
It is highly unlikely and undesirable that an information service should need to 'go it alone' in the collection of information. Such is the volume, complexity and variety of sources of information in present-day society that, unless your service has very narrow terms of

reference, it will be virtually impossible for it to collect and keep up to date all the information that is required. Therefore, it is important that you first of all identify the information providers, support services and 'gate-keepers' in your community and establish effective contacts with them. These links may already have been forged in the process of conducting a community profile. They now need to be fostered and strengthened, so that there can be a mutual exchange of information. These contacts will also be able to provide you with useful feedback from the community as to the success or otherwise of your service.

The network of contacts can be maintained on a fairly casual basis as the need arises, or you might want to formalize the arrangement. Some ways of doing this include irregular 'get togethers', informal luncheon clubs, regular meetings with agendas and minutes, or the circulation of a newsletter or bulletin. Other activities that could develop out of such meetings are joint collection of information, shared publicity, compilation and publication of directories, information handbooks and leaflets, training, and general discussion of common problems.

Collecting information is a time-consuming process and there is no one method of going about it. You will probably have to use a combination of several techniques to build up a satisfactory information base. One thing definitely to be avoided is duplicating work that has already been done. So first of all identify the following:

1 *Existing information files.* Contact all the other community information services, council departments and organizations who are likely to maintain information files and ask if they would be willing to share this information. Try to offer something in return, either an exchange of information or some other help you can provide.

2 *Local directories.* There are several types of directory that may be available in your area and which are useful sources of soft information: (a) local government authorities often produce directories or town guides of their area which contain a certain amount of local information or they may produce a guide to council services (Figure 9); (b) telephone directories, especially *Yellow pages* which have an alphabetical subject arrangement; (c) area directories, such as those produced by Thompson's Newspapers, which are similar to *Yellow pages* but also contain a section of community information – your local newspaper may produce a directory of local services, sometimes

N

NATIONAL INSURANCE see page 62 (Social Security DSS)

NATIONAL NON-DOMESTIC RATES see BUSINESS RATES

NATURE CONSERVATION see COUNTRYSIDE

NEIGHBOUR DISPUTES

Neighbours are asked to try and resolve the dispute themselves before asking the council for help.

Cambridge City North of City (0223) 463295, South of City (0223) 463232 - Housing Services

East Cambs. - no specific service

Fenland (0354) 54321 ext. 450 - Housing Management Section

Huntingdonshire - no specific service

Peterborough (0733) 317570 - Planning and Env. Health

South Cambs. - no specific service

NEIGHBOURHOOD WATCH SCHEMES

County Crime Prevention Officer (0480) 456111 ext. 2340 - Cambs. Constabulary

NOISE

Measurement, assessment and advice on all noise problems affecting people in their homes and at work.

Cambridge City (0223) 463367 - Env. Health and Protection

East Cambs. (0353) 665555 ext. 313 - Env. Health Div.

Fenland (0354) 54321 ext. 431 - Housing and Pollution Section

Huntingdonshire (0480) 456161 - Env. Health Section

Peterborough (0733) 317570 - Planning and Env. Health

South Cambs. (0223) 351795 ext. 251/255 - Env. Health Section or (0223) 351795 - Housing Section (council property)

NURSES AGENCIES

Registration of nurses agencies and monitoring of staff quality.

See TRADING STANDARDS

NURSERIES see DAY NURSERIES

NURSERY SCHOOLS

Registration of non-council nursery schools employing qualified nursery teachers and assistants.

County Under 8's Adviser See SOCIAL SERVICES

O

OCCUPATIONAL THERAPY

Therapists work alongside other Social Services staff to help in the rehabilitation of people with physical disabilities, learning disabilities or mental health problems. They assess the person's needs and may recommend special equipment or adaptations to the home to make daily life easier.

County See SOCIAL SERVICES

OFFENSIVE TRADES AND PRACTICES

Regulation and inspection of offensive trades (such as rag and bone merchants) to protect public health.

Cambridge City (0223) 463367 - Env. Health and Protection

East Cambs. (0353) 665555 ext. 291 - Env. Health Division

A Woodlands Officer checks a young tree

forty

Fig. 9 *An A–Z guide of council services provided in Cambridgeshire,* **Cambridgeshire County Council, 1992.**

in conjunction with local information groups (Figure 10); (d) citizen's guides may also be produced by the local newspaper as a supplement to an existing newspaper; (e) CVSs or RCCs sometimes produce directories of voluntary organizations in their area or you may find these listed in your local CVS/RCC annual report; (f) directories covering a special subject, such as accommodation, halls for hire, etc.; (g) directories aimed at a particular interest group or groups e.g. people with disabilities or senior citizens.

Health and hospitals (cont)

Dickens, J. J., Gofton, P. K., Joyce, M. W., Wilkinson, Anne, Wilkinson, R. M., Bradburn, Linda, Kilgallen Dr C. J., 150 Park Road, tel: 62541. By appointment 9am-5.30pm except Sat.

Fallowfield, M. G., Watson, J. D., Cathedral Square Dental Surgery, 3rd Floor Market Chambers, 1-4 Long Causeway, tel: 314131. By appointment 8.30am-5.30pm.

Lewis, K. J., Taylor, Miss J. A., Cockburn, A., White, N. B., Robert, James J., Couch, S. G., Derry, G. B., Wickham, M. A., 157 Broadway, tel: 49606. By appointment 8am-6.30pm.

Glen, J. G., 81 London Road, tel: 40005. By appointment 9am-5.30pm.

Hurford, A. E., 7 Mace Road, Stanground, tel: 66203. By appointment.

Jones, I., Marsh, K. H., Nicholls, A. F., Reynolds, J. F., 95 Lincoln Road, tel: 62436/60842. By appointment.

Livingstone, D., 63 Broadway, tel: 62394. 9.15am-5.15pm. Sat — appointments only.

Stephens, M. J. R., Trawford, D. T., Weld, J. A., Herlington Dental Centre, Orton Malborne, tel: 234566. By appointment 8am-5pm.

Wilson, C. A., Dalrymple, N. L., 63 Park Road, tel: 312532. By appointment.

MARKET DEEPING
Hein, E. C., Surgery, Bridge House, Market Deeping, tel: 342215.
Rawlings, A. P., Unit 10, Deeping Centre, tel: Market Deeping 347677.

OUNDLE
Goodman, O. C., Mumford, J. S., 36 West Street, tel: 72515.

WHITTLESEY
Connor, P. J., 5 Causeway Centre, tel: Peterborough 202587. By appointment.

Are you disabled and looking for a support group? You'll find a full list under our main heading 'Welfare, Voluntary and Environmental'.

CHIROPODY
Enquiries to Mrs J. Webster, Community Health Services, Midgate House, Midgate, Peterborough, tel: 51634 extn. 49.

CHILD HEALTH CLINICS

PETERBOROUGH
Town Hall, Peterborough, tel: 63141.
Tues 2pm-4pm.

The Clinic, Lawn Avenue Dogsthorpe, tel: 65174. Monday 2pm-4pm.

The Clinic, Mounisteven Avenue, tel: 71001. Tues 2pm-4pm.

The Clinic, 169 London Road, Old Fletton, tel: Peterborough 42564. Every Tuesday 2pm-4pm.

The Clinic, Paston Health Centre, Chadburn, tel: 72584. Tues 2pm-4pm.

The Clinic, 59 Copsewood, Werrington, tel: 78099. Wed 2pm-4pm.

Stanground Health Centre, tel: Peterborough 63848. Thurs 2pm-4pm.

Bretton Health Centre, tel: 264506. Thurs 10am-12noon.

Bushfield Health Centre, Bushfield. Orton Goldhay, tel: 238111. Thurs 10am-12 noon and 2pm-3pm.

Orton Malborne Health Centre, Herlington, tel: 233016. Tues 10am-12noon, Fri 2pm-4pm.

The Clinic, Wicken Way, Westwood, tel: Peterborough 265481. Tues 2pm-4pm.

MARKET DEEPING
Market Deeping Health Centre, 2 Douglas Road, tel: Market Deeping 342388. Wednesdays 10am-12 noon and 2pm-4pm. A doctor is available for consultation in the afternoon.

OUNDLE
Health Clinic, Glapthorne Road.
Health visitors, each day 9am-10.30am.
Mondays: ante-natal 10am-11.30am; post natal 11am-12noon; child health 2pm-4pm. Tuesdays Toddler Club 2pm-3.30pm; Thursday speech therapist 9am-12noon, tel: Oundle 73327.

WHITTLESEY
Jenner Health Centre, Turners Lane, Whittlesey, tel: Peterborough 203601.
Tues. 2pm-4pm.

FAMILY PLANNING CLINICS
Town Hall, Peterborough, tel: I eterborough 54961. First Wednesday in every month 1.45pm-3.45pm. Wednesdays 6.15pm-8.15pm. Fridays 11.30am-2.30pm.

Peterborough District Hospital (Maternity Unit, Aldermans Drive), tel: Peterborough 51634.

I.U.D. Clinic. For insertion of interuterine device. Thursdays 6.30pm-8.30pm.

Bretton Health Centre (Rightwell East, Bretton), tel: Peterborough 264656. 1st, 3rd and 5th Wednesdays 7.00pm-9.00pm. 2nd and 4th Thursdays 2pm-4pm.

Jenner Health Centre (Turners Lane, Whittlesey), tel: Peterborough 203601. 1st Thursday 5pm-7pm.

Family Planning Association.
Information officer: June Webb, 19 Thorpe Park Road, Peterborough, tel: 69140.

This local information section was compiled with the help of . . . **PETERBOROUGH INFORMATION GROUP**

Fig. 10 *EMAP trade spotter plus*, East Midlands Allied Press, 1984.

3 *National directories* are useful not only for the wider network of services but also for identifying local offices of a national organization. See p. 12 for a list of some of these and also *Printed reference material*, 3rd edn, Library Association, 1990, pp. 324–58.

Other methods to use in building up your information base and maintaining its currency include:

4 *Looking and listening.* A lot of information can be gathered by simply walking around your community, looking at noticeboards, picking up leaflets, or attending open meetings, fairs, fêtes and other community events. This method of collecting information is unpredictable and requires more than a 9-to-5, five-day week.

5 *Contact with individuals.* People are a major source of information in any community and there are always those to whom others naturally go for information. Try to identify such people and enlist their help, possibly by offering something in return – bartering is a time-honoured system! Direct contact with individuals in other information services and organizations is often a better way of eliciting information than impersonal methods and also paves the way for further cooperation. Pay regular visits to such centres.

6 *Scanning newspapers, magazines, newsletters, etc.* can turn up details of new organizations; changes of personnel, premises or hours of opening; new services introduced; and may highlight problem areas where information may be needed.

7 *Other documents,* including council minutes and agendas, planning regulations, annual reports (ask to be put on mailing lists for these), leaflets and manifestos.

8 *Media publicity.* Local press, radio and cable television stations may be prepared without charge to put out a call for organizations to contact your service. If not, then consider inserting an advert or, where there is a local directory produced, have a tear-out slip included for organizations to fill in and return to you.

As a result of these various methods, an amount of raw material will have been obtained which may be of use to your information service. How accurate, up to date and complete the data is will depend very much on the reliability of the source. In most cases, unless you have every confidence in the source, the information will have to be checked before it is entered in a more permanent form in your resource file. So, at this stage, simply record it onto say a scrap

5in × 3in card and put it into a temporary file.

The information you have obtained will be of several different kinds but the most common will probably be that relating to organizations, clubs and societies. This is the most difficult type of information to collect since it is ever changing and therefore unrelenting effort will be required to achieve even reasonable completeness or accuracy – 100% will be impossible. However, with a good system for collecting and updating the information, you should be able to build up and maintain an acceptable file. A lot of staff time will be needed to carry out this work, so first of all investigate whether there are other local information services that need this type of information and would be willing to help in its collection. It may be possible to collect the information through an umbrella group, where the work can be farmed out so that it is not too great a burden on any one organization. Alternatively, a joint approach can be made on behalf of a number of organizations.

Ideally, the most effective way to collect information of this kind is to pay a personal visit to each organization or service, but rarely will that be possible without extensive staff resources or a very small community. The cheapest and quickest way to collect this information is by telephoning. Prepare a standard list of questions to ask so that entries in your information file follow the same format. Telephoning is only practicable if you have a reasonably small number of organizations to contact, say up to one hundred. If visits and telephoning are ruled out, then the information can be collected initially by postal questionnaire, with a request for up-to-date information sent at least once a year and also when it is known from other sources that changes have taken place. A covering letter should be sent with the questionnaire or update request, explaining why the information is needed and asking for cooperation. If the information is to be passed on to other organizations or commercial bodies, either free or for payment, this should be drawn to the attention of the recipient of the questionnaire so that they have an opportunity to decline to give the information or insist that it is not so disseminated. If the information is to be stored in a computer, then you will need to meet the requirements of the Data Protection Act. A free booklet describing the requirements of the Act can be obtained from Office of the Data Protection Registrar, Springfield House, Water Lane, Wilmslow, Cheshire SK9 5AX (Tel. 0625-535777).

If it can be afforded, include with your questionnaire some means of returning it free of charge, as this will significantly improve the response rate. Separate forms may be required to collect different kinds of information. The following is a suggested list of headings which you might need to include on forms for collecting information from two of the most common types of organization.

Clubs and societies
- *Name*: the name by which the club is best known, plus the full name if different. Indicate relationship to larger body, i.e. branch, regiment, lodge, etc.
- *Secretary's name, address and telephone number* or those of a similar person if the organization has no secretary.
- *Place, day and time of meetings.*
- *Purpose of organization* if not self-evident from the name.
- *Eligibility*: any restrictions by age, sex, ethnic group, occupation, status (single, divorced, widowed) etc.
- *Subscription*: any charge to become a member or to attend meetings.
- *Annual general meeting*: the date of an organization's AGM can be a useful indication of when to send out update forms as this is when officers or policies are likely to change.
- *Other officers*: names, addresses, telephone numbers of treasurer, president, chairman, publicity officer, membership secretary, etc.
- *History of the organization* including special events or persons associated with it.
- *Publications*: newsletter, diary, commemorative brochures, annual report, etc.
- *Date* the information was obtained and/or last updated or checked.

Agencies and organizations providing a service
- *Name*: popular name and full name, e.g. CHAT (Come Here and Talk), SHAC (Shelter Housing Action Centre), plus relationship to parent body where necessary.
- *Address*: street address and postal address, Post Office box number if used.
- *Telephone and fax number*, including service number, administration number, after-hours or hotline numbers.
- *Contact person*: personal name, title and address, if different from above.

- *Hours of opening*: days and times; note if seasonal, e.g. holiday period, term time.
- *Services provided*: advice, counselling, practical help, etc.; types of enquiry the service would like to have referred to them.
- *Eligibility*: age, income, sex, residency, status.
- *Application procedures*: walk-in, appointment or waiting list; what papers or documents need to be brought.
- *Cost*: free, fees, means-tested, donations; any facilities for payments to be spread over a period; help available from local or central government, charities, etc.
- *Geographical area served*: neighbourhood, city, county, region, *ad hoc* area; no geographical restrictions.
- *Branch offices*: extension bureaux, mobiles, surgeries, etc.; include hours of opening, routes and times of stops.
- *Director*, administrator or executive director of the service; name and telephone or extension.
- *Volunteers*: does the service use volunteers and for what purposes? Method of recruitment.
- *Publications*: directories, handbooks, leaflets, annual report, etc.
- *Funding*: local government grant-aided, donations, etc.
- *Special facilities*: foreign languages spoken, access and facilities for people with disabilities, photocopying or fax service, escort, advocacy, etc.
- *Transportation*: how to get to the service, e.g. bus route numbers, underground line and station, etc.
- *Date* information was obtained and/or last updated or checked.

These two lists represent most of the facts that a community information service might need to know about an organization or service. In practice, depending on the scope of your service, it may not be necessary to include all the fields in the questionnaire. It is a good idea to get the person filling in the questionnaire to sign it, thereby giving the information service some protection against claims of giving out wrong information – a not uncommon occurrence, especially when the information is committed to print.

There are other types of 'soft' information that your service might need to collect, for example halls for hire, places of local worship, accommodation, 'What's-on' events, local industry. The procedure is much the same:

- Decide what information you need to know.
- Devise a standard format or list of questions to ask.
- Identify possible sources of information.
- Decide which method or methods to use to collect the information: telephone, personal visit, postal questionnaire, press advert, etc.

How to store 'soft' information
There are various methods that can be used for storing information:

1 A *list* is easy and quick to consult, can be photocopied for clients to take away and can be faxed, but has very little flexibility for inserting and updating information.

2 A *strip index* provides flexibility, can easily be photocopied, and is available in various forms: large binders holding many pages, smaller folders containing just a few pages, address books, wall-hung panels, rotunda units, etc. Strips are available in several colours, which allows for a simple categorization, and various widths. Even so, they are limited as to the amount of information that can be contained on them. It is also not quite as easy to insert new strips as the manufacturers claim.

3 *Cards* are still one of the most commonly used systems for storing information. They are infinitely flexible, easy to insert and update, can be sorted into any preferred order, and require very little technical know-how. The most popular sizes are 5in × 3in, used mainly for indexes or temporary information waiting to be checked, 6in × 4in, and 8in × 5in, which are large enough to contain sufficient information about most organizations or services and to be pre-printed with a standard grid for recording the information. There are more superior types of card file available, such as the Rondofile or Rotadex systems (see pp. 34–6) which use custom-designed stationery and therefore tend to be more expensive. With systems that use standard cards, you can – if you are hard-up or want to save trees – use the reverse of scrap cards. Card files have a number of disadvantages: they are not so easy to carry around, they are not easily reproducible if someone wants a copy of a particular section, multiple access (e.g. by name, subject, area, service, etc.) requires duplication of cards, and the updating process can be tedious.

You may still find around *edge-punched cards* which offer a primitive type of multi-access to the information on the card through the strategic use of knitting needles or rods. Personally, I would save up and get a computer.

4 *Loose-leaf binders* with one sheet for each entry, sometimes called 'sheaf' binders, have a similar flexibility to cards. They are slightly slower to add to and amend but are more portable. They are suited best for alphabetical arrangements as they are difficult to guide.

5 *Microcomputers* now have the capacity to handle immense information files that can be accessed by any number of predetermined variables or even free-text searching by keyword, depending on the software used. With a printer attached, all the information or sections of it can be printed out on demand or to provide a master for printing by conventional methods. Personal computers now begin at prices that bring them within the range of most community information services. However, there is danger in automatically seeing the computer as the best solution for maintaining your information file, as this may not always be the case. A lot depends on the size of your file and its complexity, what you want to do with the file, and to what other uses you want to put the computer. The importance of the computer in information and advice work is such that it merits a chapter to itself, and you will find these and other aspects dealt with in more detail in Chapter Eight.

Filing system

Whichever method is chosen for physically storing the information, except for that by microcomputer, it will be necessary to decide the best way of arranging entries so that the information can be retrieved swiftly and accurately. In order to ensure that the total resources of your information service are used to the full when answering an enquiry, it will help if the system used to organize the information file can be integrated with that for the vertical file and the bookstock. This point needs to be borne in mind now, although it will be dealt with more fully later.

The bulk of the information file is likely to comprise 'soft' information which you have collected about organizations, clubs, societies and services and, to a lesser extent, about individuals who are a valuable source of information or advice, plus items of 'hard' information not available or conveniently available in printed form. There are several ways in which you might want to retrieve this information

– by the names of the organizations, by subject (i.e. area of interest), by clientele, by the type of service (e.g. counselling), or by place. In practice, the 'clientele' and 'type of service' approaches are usually catered for through the subject file rather than as separate files.

Organizations file

The master file for the whole system will usually be an alphabetically arranged sequence of entries by name of organization. It is generally recommended that the full, official name of the organization is used, with references from other forms of the name. In practice, it does not really matter as long as there are references from the alternatives to whichever form is chosen. There is a good argument for putting the main entry for an organization under the form of name by which most people refer to it, even if this differs from or is an abbreviation of the official name. This is especially so where the file is to be used by the public.

Where many of the organizations begin with the same word (e.g. a place name), you may prefer to invert the heading e.g. ROSE SOCI-ETY, BLANKVILLE. Some people frown on inverted headings but they can be a useful way of introducing a kind of subject arrange-ment into what is basically a name file, for example:

BLIND, ROYAL NATIONAL INSTITUTE FOR THE - Blankville Branch
BLIND, SUNSHINE CLUB FOR THE
BLIND, TALKING NEWSPAPER FOR THE

You will need to refer from the uninverted form of the name, for example:

SUNSHINE CLUB FOR THE BLIND
see BLIND, SUNSHINE CLUB FOR THE

This only works, of course, for those organizations whose names indicate their sphere of activities.

In addition to details of organizations, each entry in the master file may also contain certain 'housekeeping' details relating to the maintenance of all the information files (see pp. 70–1), plus refer-ences to appropriate headings in the subject file, where relevant information can be found, and a classification number (see pp. 81–3).

Subject file

Most enquiries received by a community information service are likely to be about the need for a service or activity or for help with solving a problem, rather than for information on a specific named organization. So the information you have collected about organizations, services and individuals will also need to be accessible by the services and activities they provide. There are two ways this can be achieved, by either using a subject index or having a subject file of organizations. In both, you will need to choose or adopt a set of subject headings which will adequately describe the information on file or elsewhere in the system and the interests of your clientele.

If you are compiling your own list of subject headings, choose terms that are in common use by your clientele, especially if they will be consulting the files directly, rather than the 'official' term, e.g OUT OF WORK or ON THE DOLE instead of REDUNDANT. Always refer from alternatives not used to the chosen term.

A *subject index* is rather like the index to a book. It is an alphabetically arranged file of subject heading cards on which reference is made to where information on that subject can be found. The cards themselves do not contain information. The subject index can contain references to organizations, individuals and other supplementary material, such as pamphlets, periodical articles, audiovisual material, books, etc. (see Figure 11).

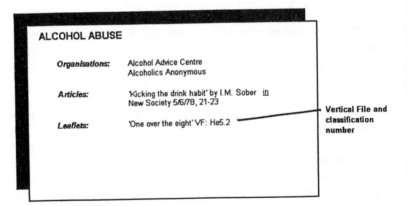

ALCOHOL ABUSE

Organisations:	Alcohol Advice Centre
	Alcoholics Anonymous
Articles:	'Kicking the drink habit' by I.M. Sober in
	New Society 5/6/78, 21-23
Leaflets:	'One over the eight' VF: He5.2

Vertical File and classification number

Fig. 11 Subject index card.

A *subject file* consists of an alphabetically arranged set of subject heading cards behind which are filed copies of the organization cards appropriate to that heading and possibly cards containing items of 'hard' information. An alternative is to arrange cards according to a classification system either devised by yourself or adopted from another service, such as the NACAB classification scheme (see p. 83).

Place file

Where an information service covers a number of distinct towns, villages or neighbourhoods, each having a similar range of organizations, it may be helpful to have a file that can be accessed by place. There are a number of options. You could sort the organizations file initially by place, especially if it contains few organizations whose responsibilities extend to the whole area covered by your service.

Alternatively, if most of the organizations are prefixed with the name of the place (e.g. EXVILLE ATHLETIC CLUB, EXVILLE COUNCIL FOR THE DISABLED), the alphabetically arranged master file will automatically bring together those from the same location, provided inverted headings have not been used. Some arrangements will have to be made for organizations which do not conform to the pattern, either because the place-name does not feature at the beginning or because it is not contained in the name of the organization at all. In these cases, an additional card can be made out with either an inverted heading (e.g. EXVILLE, ROTARY CLUB OF) or the place-name can be prefixed (e.g. EXVILLE – 20/30 CLUB).

The third option is to have a separate file of organization cards arranged initially by place and then alphabetically by name of organization or by subject.

Filing alphabetically

Filing alphabetically is not quite as simple as ABC, as any librarian will tell you. There are two recognized methods, known as 'word by word' and 'letter by letter'. In word by word, entries are initially sorted by the first word in the heading, then headings that begin with the same word are sorted by the second word and so on. Another way to describe this method, which may be more helpful, is to treat spaces between words in a heading as an imaginary letter coming before 'a' in the alphabet, then sort letter by letter.

In letter by letter, you simply ignore any spaces in the heading and sort one letter at a time from left to right. Here is how a small group of headings would look sorted by the two methods:

Word by word	*Letter by letter*
DO SOMETHING! BOYS CLUB	'DOG AND BONE' DARTS TEAM
'DOG AND BONE' DARTS TEAM	DOGSBURY RESIDENTS'
DOG SNIFFERS ANONYMOUS	ASSOCIATION
DOGS HOMES	DOGS HOMES
DOGSBURY RESIDENTS'	DOG SNIFFERS ANONYMOUS
ASSOCIATION	DO SOMETHING! BOYS CLUB

There are several other niceties to do with filing alphabetically but I only need mention here that hyphens are treated as spaces in word-by-word sorting and numerals are spelt out as said, so that 1900 (the year) is considered for sorting as NINETEEN HUNDRED and 1,900 as ONE THOUSAND, NINE HUNDRED.

File 'housekeeping'

In addition to the information needed to answer enquiries, there are other items of information to do with the maintenance of the file which may usefully be included on each entry, such as the following:

● the date the information was obtained, last updated or last checked, which will indicate not only the degree of reliability to be placed on it but also when to update (see below);
● the date a questionnaire or update letter was sent – a check for chasing up non-returned forms;
● additional contacts or other information which does not fit into the main part of the entry;
● subject headings used in the subject file;
● place headings used in the place file, if not obvious from the name of the organization;
● feedback – comments from users of the service;
● 'tracings', i.e. a list of other cards that refer to that entry, so that they can be traced and amended or withdrawn when necessary.

The amount of this 'housekeeping' information you need to include will depend on how sophisticated you need your file to be. The bigger the information service and the larger the file, then the more likely it is that you will need to introduce a systematic procedure for processing information. In such a case it is usual for the housekeeping information to go on the reverse of each entry, using a standard grid like the one illustrated here (Figure 12). It is arguable that if your information file requires this degree of sophistication, you ought seriously to consider keeping it on computer.

For a small community information service, it may be quite adequate just to note the date when the information was collected, checked or updated.

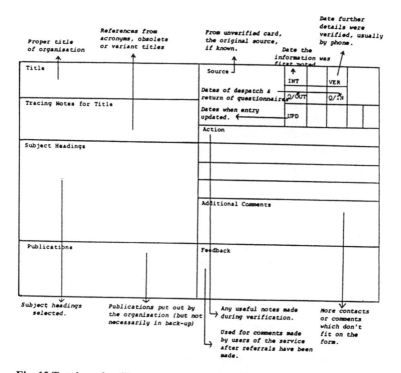

Fig. 12 Tracings for file maintenance (from Keehan, Anne L. and Riatti, Catherine, *Establishing a local community information service. Part 1: Guidelines for development and maintenance*, Library Board of Western Australia, 1982, p.42).

Updating

By their very nature the entries in your database will be changing continually. Hours of opening, meeting places, officers, membership fees, subscriptions, charges, etc. are all susceptible to frequent change. Therefore, it is important to have a system for regularly updating each entry in the database. There are several ways of achieving this but, whichever method you adopt, it must be regular and ongoing.

Interim updating

All the entries for organizations should be checked at least once a year to ensure they are still correct. In between times, however, new information will be brought to your attention by various means, including word of mouth, newspaper reports, organization newsletters, company reports and by direct contact with the organization itself. If the source of information is reliable, it can be substituted immediately for the out-of-date information in the database but, if not, it should be noted and a further check made to verify its accuracy. A simple way to add new information to an entry in a card file is to write it onto self-adhesive labels or slips (obtainable at most stationers) which can be stuck over the original information. Even though an entry has been updated in between times, it should still be checked formally once a year.

Annual updating

Once a year is probably a reasonable time-span for updating your database but a shorter interval may be necessary if the information content changes frequently. You will need to decide how the annual update is to be carried out. Some organizations like to update the entire file at the same time, so that they can say the file was as accurate as possible at a particular date. However, this does create a tremendous amount of extra work for a period of several weeks, and you may feel it necessary to get extra paid, work-experience or volunteer help. Another disadvantage of this method is that it captures a picture of organizations at a set moment in time. Some organizations may be just about to make changes, and your records for these would be out of date for almost a year.

Alternatively, you may decide to update on a continuous basis by using either the date the record was added to the database or the organization's annual general meeting (AGM) date as a trigger. This is easy to do if your database is kept on a computer, since a date field can be used to produce a subset of records and, by linking the database with a word processing package, a personalized standard letter can be printed out for sending to each organization. It is less easy with a card or any other kind of file. You can get little coloured metal tags to clip on to the top edge of cards, a different colour for each month, or you could use an appropriate symbol on the heading of the card, such as a coloured dot, a letter or number. Tags can make the file look a bit messy and are easily knocked off if it is in constant use; symbols require the whole file to be checked through.

My preference is to update records shortly before or after each organization's AGM, since most organizations, if they are going to change their officers or constitution, generally do it once a year at the AGM. As many organizations do not know their AGM date a year in advance, it is enough just to indicate the month in which the AGM is usually held. For those organizations and services which do not have an AGM, you will need to use the date the information was added as the trigger.

When writing to organizations to update their information, it is better to send them a copy of their record with a request to indicate any changes, rather than sending a blank questionnaire. This saves the secretary unnecessary time in repeating information that has not altered.

An alternative to writing to each organization is to phone, but this is time-consuming and costly, and only feasible if the number of organizations to contact is fairly small.

Avoid sending out updates at times when people are likely to be away, such as during the summer. There are certain times when it is more appropriate to update other kinds of information, e.g. social security benefit rates (which usually change in April and September), adult education classes or school, college and university courses which change termly.

When an updated entry is returned it should be checked to see if the subject or place headings still apply. Minor changes can be recorded on the master card and any other cards in subject or place files; major changes may require a new set of cards to be produced. For those with computerized databases the process is simpler as just the one record has to be updated. Don't forget to change the date the information was last checked or updated.

'Hard' information

As well as the database, most information services will need a certain amount of 'hard' information to answer enquiries. Short, unrecorded or inadequately recorded items of 'hard' information, as we have already seen, can be incorporated into the database. However, the majority of hard information will usually be found in one or more of the vast range of print forms, starting from locally produced free broadsheets to extremely expensive multi-volumed loose-leaf reference works. Within the scope of this book, it is not possible to go into detail about the sources of this material, since they will vary considerably according to the type and subject range of the service you are operating. Community information dates rapidly so any printed sources should be treated with care. However, you might find useful a chapter on the sources of community information that I contributed to *Printed reference material and related sources of information*, 3rd edn, Library Association Publishing, 1990, which concentrated on organizations and on those items which are regularly updated.

The following framework for collecting community information was originally devised by Grainne Morby, who at the time was working for the Community Information Project, with some additions of my own:

Distinguish between subject areas

In other words, identify the main topics into which the subject scope of your information service naturally divides.

Throughout this framework I will take as an example an information service for which the main area of interest is housing. It is sometimes useful to apply a consistent criterion when dividing up a subject, although obviously this would not be so easy for an information service whose scope covers as broad an area as, say, 'community information'. However, taking housing as our example, you could decide to divide it by type of accommodation, e.g. owner-occupied, private-rented, council-rented, New Town, Housing Association, institutional accommodation, tied accommodation, mobile homes, etc. In most cases you would probably need an additional category for subjects that cut across all or more than one category. In the case of housing, this might be 'squatting' or 'homelessness'.

What are the information needs of specific client-groups within the subject areas?

Since the material you want to collect will usually be written to meet a particular need or needs, it is advisable to collect information around those needs rather than for fitting into a theoretical framework. The kind of broad client groups that might be identified in the field of housing are landlords, tenants, owner-occupiers, squatters, transients, elderly people, people with disabilities, the homeless. Then, one could identify client groups who share a common problem or need associated with their particular type of accommodation, such as eviction, dampness, house repair, renovation, harassment, mortgages, rent arrears, planning permission, redevelopment, etc.

Once these subject areas and client needs have been identified, it should give you clearer guidelines when you come to select material from the various sources identified in the next part of the framework.

Print sources
  1 Official
    (a) National
- Pre-legislation: political party manifestos and policy documents, speeches by Ministers, the Queen's Speech at opening of Parliament, White Papers, Green Papers.
- Legislation: Bills, Hansard reports of debates in both Houses of Parliament, Acts, Statutory Instruments.
- Guidance to local statutory bodies: circulars and letters from Ministers, guidance notes, reports of Inspectors.
- Reference books: collections of legislation, e.g. *Statutes in force, Legal aid handbook.*
- Periodicals from government departments and agencies, e.g. *Department for Employment gazette.*
- Guidance to the public: leaflets, posters, videos and other A/V material.
- Ombudsmen.

    (b) Regional
- Health authorities, British Rail.
- Privatized utilities: gas, water, electricity, telephone.
- Consumer watchdog bodies: Post Office Users' National Council (POUNC), Office of Gas Supply (OFGAS), Office of Electricty Regulation (OFFER), Office of Telecommunications (OfTel), Office of Water Services (OFWAT).

(c) Local
- Local authority policies and decisions: agendas, minutes, standing orders, by-laws and regulations.
- Guidance to the public: handbooks, leaflets, etc. from local authorities, area and district health authorities, Community Health Councils, local offices of government agencies.

2 Non-official
  (a) National
- Reference books and handbooks from commercial publishers.
- Voluntary organizations.
- Pressure groups, self-help groups.
- 'Umbrella' organizations, e.g. National Council for Voluntary Organizations, Federation of Independent Advice Centres.
- Professional bodies, e.g. The Law Society.
- Trade associations, e.g. National Association of Retail Furnishers.
- Educational bodies, e.g. National Extension College, Open University.
- Trade unions.
- The media.
- Practitioners in the field who publish.

  (b) Local
- Claimants' unions.
- Law centres, other specialist advice centres.
- Neighbourhood and generalist advice centres, resource centres.
- Local 'umbrella' groups.
- Pressure groups, campaigning groups, action centres.
- Voluntary organizations.
- Local media: newspapers, community newspapers, radio, cable television.

  (c) New technology
- Videotext systems: Prestel, teletext, private viewdata.
- Online computer databases, e.g. Volnet.
- CD-ROM, videodiscs, etc.

This list is not intended to be exhaustive but will give you some idea of the range of sources in which to look for information. Howard Matthews, in his book *Community information* (Association of Assistant Librarians, 1988, 27–8) has drawn up a set of criteria for selecting community information materials. It is aimed particularly at library community information services but may be generally helpful for anyone setting up such a service.

1. Selection should be done by those who know the community best.
2. Material should relate to specific, local, identified needs.
3. All material should be current.
4. All material should be written at a level appropriate to its intended use.
5. Material should be concerned with the practicalities of problem solving.
6. All new material should either fill a gap, offer a new viewpoint, or promise something better.
7. Material should take into account the level of use the client will make of it.

Obtaining publications and other material

Once the material you require has been identified, you will need to obtain it. Some material will be priced, in which case you will need to order it, and some will be free.

Priced publications

The procedure for obtaining priced publications, particularly in the field of community information, is not as simple as you might suppose. Since a lot of the material may well be fairly cheap and from small or community publishers, booksellers and library suppliers are reluctant to obtain it as the profit margin is likely to be too low for the amount of effort involved. The alternative is to order direct but this also has its difficulties as many small publishers now insist on money with order, and this can cause problems for some organizations through the need to raise a cheque or limitations on the amount that can be spent from petty cash. A few national voluntary organizations, e.g. Age Concern England, operate a standing-order system for their publications – this is one solution, although you may need to accept blanket coverage of the organization's output. In the larger cities, you may find a community or alternative bookseller who is prepared to supply this material to order. A directory of alternative bookshops is published annually by the magazine *Radical bookseller*.

Whatever the method of ordering, it is important to keep a record of what has been placed on order and from whom to avoid duplication of titles and as a check on supply. For each title make out an order or slip – this can be either a scrap 5in × 3in card or one specially printed with a standard grid. The following indicates the kinds of information that need to be recorded:

- title of publication – more important than author for this kind of material, since authorship is often unclear;
- author – might be an individual or an organization;
- price, date of publication and, if a periodical, frequency;
- supplier – this may be a bookseller, library supplier or the address of the producing body;
- date of order;
- source of information about the item;
- location, if you are ordering for more than one centre.

You may find it helpful to use the order cards later as the basis of a catalogue of the publications in your information centre; in which case, leave space at the top of the card for either a subject heading, classification number or filing code.

After an order has been placed with a supplier, the order cards are filed, preferably by title, in one alphabetical sequence known as the 'order file'. When a publication is received, the order card is removed from the file and accompanies the publication to the next stage if it is to be used later as the catalogue card. If not, you may find it useful to file the order card in a 'publications received' file, until such time as the publication is permanently recorded in the system, after which the card can be thrown away.

Periodicals
Publications which arrive at regular intervals – weekly, fortnightly, monthly, quarterly – will not require an order card but you will need to keep a record of each title taken. This should include the following items of information:

- title of periodical;
- frequency;
- supplier;

- when subscription is due for payment;
- a grid to record receipt of each issue;
- instructions for disposal of back copies.

For those using computers, there are software packages available for periodicals management but these are aimed at organizations who take an extensive range of periodicals and such packages are not cheap. If you have a database management package on your computer, you would do better to devise your own periodicals database.

Free material

This can vary from quite substantial loose-leaf binders plus updates to leaflets, posters and bookmarks and may be required in bulk for clients to take. Since this is likely to be a frequent type of request, it may be quicker and simpler to duplicate a standard letter to send to organizations, with space left to fill in address, title of item, format (leaflet, booklet, poster, etc.) and number of copies required. It is advisable to keep a record of what is requested, if only as a check on whether it has been received or not. Where you are ordering in bulk for several centres, a card or slip such as that shown here (Figure 13)

LEAFLET REQUEST SLIP		DATE ORDERED			
TITLE OF LEAFLET					
		NUMBER OF COPIES			
NAME AND ADDRESS OF SUPPLIER		DISTRIBUTION			
		B		SW	
		D		Th	
		E		We	
		F		Wh	
CENTRE	NUMBER REQUIRED	O		Wi	
		St		Y	

Fig. 13 Leaflet request slip for centralized ordering for system of 12 libraries.

79

can serve as a request slip for each centre, the order record and, when copies are received, the distribution record. You should file cards for free materials either in the order file or in a separate section.

A lot of the sweat has been taken out of identifying free materials, and addresses from where they can be obtained, through the setting-up of Camden Libraries' Free Leaflets Information Service (FLIS). For an annual fee (£120 in 1992) subscribers receive a copy of the *Frills* directory of free information leaflet suppliers, a monthly batch of new and updated leaflets and amendments to the *Frills* directory, and details of a model system for organizing leaflets. Details of this service can be obtained from Community Information Services, Camden Leisure Services Department, St Pancras Library, 100 Euston Road, London NW1 2AJ. A similar, but not so extensive, service is provided by the NACAB as part of its Information Service, but you would need to have approval to subscribe to the full pack (see pp. 93–5 for prices as at 1992).

Organizing hard information

We have already seen that hard information can be found in a great variety of forms. For the benefit of organizing it, the following categories can be identified:

1 *Material in book form* for use by clientele or information workers will be best arranged on shelves in the broad subject groups identified when acquiring the material (see pp. 74–5) or according to a classification scheme (see below).

2 *Ephemeral material for use by information workers* is best stored in a vertical file using the same subject headings as those in the subject sequence of the information file, though probably with more subdivisions, or using a classification scheme. Alternatively, the material could be kept in file boxes on shelves using broad subject headings.

3 *Ephemeral material for use by clientele on the premises* is best kept in file boxes, ring or display binders and ideally interfiled with books. Vertical files are not recommended for public use as they tend to be a deterrent. Another way of dealing with ephemeral materials is to gather them together in packs on particular topics (see pp. 110–12 and, for maximum impact, to display them face outwards on sloping shelves.

4 *Ephemeral material for the public to take away* can be displayed

in special leaflet dispensers, on a sloping surface or on tables. Ideally, they should be displayed in broad subject groups or by originating organization, e.g. Benefits Agency, Department for Employment, but this is rarely possible because even within organizations leaflets are produced in varying sizes.

Supplementary information

Many organizations produce printed material in the course of their work or activities. The most common types of material are directories or address lists of members (individuals or constituent groups), newsletters, events sheets or cards, annual reports, constitutions, posters, leaflets, funding appeals, campaigning literature, advertising brochures, balance sheets and commemorative booklets (anniversaries, etc.). All this material is potentially useful as back-up information to the database but there is no sure way of obtaining it. When sending out the original questionnaire to organizations, you can ask to be put on their mailing list for this type of material, if one is maintained. Some organizations that operate on a shoestring may make a small charge for their mailing list facility. Even when you are put on a mailing list, regular receipt of material may depend very much on the enthusiasm or efficiency of the secretary of an organization. Often the best solution to obtaining material is to maintain regular contact with organizations and to pester them continually.

When material arrives, it should be dated, so that you know roughly how old it is, and carefully filed for future use. The simplest method is to have an envelope or folder for each organization. Write on the outside of the envelope the name of the organization as used in your database and arrange envelopes alphabetically in boxes or a vertical file. You should also add to this file any cuttings from newspapers or magazines concerning those organizations. The file should be checked regularly, at least once a year, to remove out-of-date material. When writing to organizations for updated information for your database, ask them for any new literature.

Before throwing away the withdrawn material, check to see if it would be of use to some other organization or section of your service which collects material on local history.

Classification

It is not my intention to go into any great detail about the classification of community information materials. For most small information services, it will be quite adequate to arrange material by broad subject groups subdivided according to the form in which the clientele's needs and problems are presented. For ease of labelling vertical files, book spines and boxes, a simple notation can be used based on the initial letter or letters of subjects. For example, Cambridgeshire Libraries' community information service covers 21 categories:

Ben	Benefits	**Gov**	Government
Bus	Business	**Hea**	Health
Car	Careers	**Hou**	Housing
Com	Community	**Law**	Legal rights
Con	Consumer	**Mon**	Money
CR	Community relations	**SC**	Senior citizens
Dis	Disability	**Tra**	Transport
Edu	Education	**Ump**	Unemployment
Emp	Employment	**Wom**	Women
Env	Environment	**You**	Youth
Fam	Family		

Some libraries also include as separate categories: Death, Equal opportunities, Fuel (or Energy), Gay rights, Leisure, and Trade union rights. These categories can then be broken down into smaller sub-categories as necessary. Taking the earlier example of Housing, a possible range of subcategories with a mnemonic notation might be:

A	Agricultural accommodation	**Re**	Rented accommodation
H	Homelessness	**ReC**	Council housing
I	Institutional accommodation	**ReH**	Housing Association housing
M	Mobile homes	**ReP**	Private rented
O	Owner-occupied	**S**	Squatting

Numerals could be introduced for more detailed subdivisions, e.g .O1 – Buying and selling a house; O2 – Home insurance; O3 – Planning applications; O4 – Development; etc.

An effective method that can be used where you have only a small number of broad categories (no more than ten and preferably less) is colour coding. Allocate a colour to each subject and attach an appropriate coloured sticker or tape to the spine of each book or file box. Colour coding can be used in conjunction with notation to provide more detailed subdivision of a subject.

When a community information service grows to a size where

broad categories are not adequate to contain all the material and allow efficient retrieval, then it may be necessary to consider using a classification scheme. Two choices are open to you, either using or adapting a ready-made scheme or constructing your own. There are a number of general classification schemes used in libraries, of which the most well known is the Dewey Decimal Classification. These schemes have been constructed to organize the whole of knowledge and subjects are usually arranged on philosophical or logical princi-ples. Consequently, they may not be sufficiently detailed or treat subjects in the way your clientele express their information needs. Most schemes have a degree of flexibility and it might be possible to adapt them. The NACAB has its own scheme for arranging materials in the broad area of community information, but it hardly merits the description of a classification scheme. However, it is sufficiently detailed and client oriented to be worthy of consideration. It is less strong on areas of support material, e.g. for groups or self-help health. The 14 broad categories of this scheme are:

1	Communications	8	Family and Personal
2	Travel, Transport	9	Social Security
3	Immigration and Nationality	10	Health
4	Administration of Justice	11	Housing
5	Education	12	Taxes and Duties
6	Employment	13	Consumer
7	National and International	14	Leisure

Constructing your own classification scheme is not a task to be entered into lightly and it is certainly not within the scope of this basic guide to describe how to go about it. If you would like to try this, I can refer you to a booklet produced by the Community Infor-mation Service of the Northern Ireland Council of Social Service (now Northern Ireland Council for Voluntary Action), which you may still be able to get hold of, called *Designing a community information system* (NICVA, 127 Ormeau Road, Belfast BT7 1SH, 1980). This describes, step by step, the process they went through in constructing a classification scheme to meet their own needs. The scheme is also reproduced in the booklet.

The parts of this chapter on organizing information have of neces-sity been kept as simple and as brief as possible. A more detailed approach to the subject will be found in *Organizing information: principles and practice*, by Chris Turner (Library Association Pub-lishing, 1986, £18.50, pb £14.80).

Chapter Five

Giving out information

Once you have built up the information base of your service, then the next step is to consider how that information is to be made available to potential users of the service. There are a number of possibilities as follows:

- face-to-face contact with clients;
- by telephone;
- postal requests;
- by display;
- selective dissemination of the information (SDI);
- indirectly to clients through deposit files;
- through publications
  - to other information workers, professionals or groups
  - to clientele;
- information packs;
- online;
- through the media.

Not every information service will want or need to adopt all these methods. It may be that, when assessing the need for your service, there was a clear indication of which method of dissemination would be most appropriate. Nevertheless, it is worth exploring other means, since the effectiveness of your service should be constantly under review and it may be that more people could be reached by adopting a new or additional method of dissemination.

Face-to-face contact with clientele
This is the passive function, whereby a community information service is located in a particular building or room and the clientele call in person to seek information for themselves or from the staff by

enquiry at an information desk. It has the advantages that the most up-to-date information is available, provided the service has carried out its information-gathering efficiently; the client can be questioned to reveal exactly what information is required; and a member of staff familiar with using the files or databases is on hand to search out information, to make contact with services, or to suggest further possible courses of action. There is some evidence to suggest that many people prefer information to be transmitted verbally, especially if they have low literacy skills.

Some disadvantages to having one defined location are that, unless it is prominently sited (in the High Street or shopping centre), it may be difficult to bring the service to the attention of potential users without a continual publicity campaign; moreover, it can be expensive to operate in terms of the resources needed to staff the enquiry desk continually and to stay open outside normal office hours.

Dealing with people face-to-face requires a certain amount of skill but, above all, is needed a pleasant and approachable personality, a characteristic that is not so easily learnt. The following guidelines may be helpful in dealing with clients:

1 First of all, try to make the enquirer feel at ease, so that s/he is not afraid to ask questions or discuss a problem. It may seem a trivial enquiry to you but could be causing the client much anxiety.

2 Do not exhibit feelings of shock, horror, amusement, disbelief or repugnance at anything the enquirer says. It is not part of your job to pass judgment on a client whose behaviour or ideas are contrary to the norms of society.

3 Listen to the whole query and don't start jumping to conclusions before the enquirer has finished. Listen 'actively' by asking appropriate questions to clarify what is specifically being asked, since most people tend to phrase their questions in general terms. What the client seems to want may not necessarily be what s/he needs.

4 When you think you know what is being requested, state it in simple terms so that the enquirer can confirm that you are on the right track. I once spent ages looking through modern dance manuals to answer a request for information on 'how to jive' only to find, after proudly presenting a suitable book, that the enquirer had a speech impediment and really wanted to know 'how to djive a car'!

5 Try to identify with the enquirer's problem, at the same time remaining impartial and emotionally uninvolved. Such a counsel of

perfection is probably unattainable but is only a warning that sometimes people ask the impossible or want confirmation or support for a course of action when they are in the wrong. Even where a service sets out to be impartial, it cannot support clients irrespective of whether they are right or wrong. It may be necessary at times to give information or advice that is contrary to what the client expects to hear.

6 Before any information is given it should, wherever possible, be double-checked to ensure that it is correct and, if reasonably brief, written down to give to the client.

7 Where there are alternative courses of action, explain these to the client in simple terms and leave her/him to make the choice unless you are specifically offering an advice service.

8 Never leave the client with a negative response even when you cannot answer the query. Suggest where else the client may go to find an answer, even making a telephone call, if necessary, to fix an appointment or make an introduction. If the enquiry needs further investigation and is not urgent, take down the details and offer to phone or write with the answer as soon as possible. Suggest that the enquirer calls back after a certain interval if they have not had a reply.

By telephone

The facility to transmit information by telephone can be an advantage, especially where clientele have difficulty in reaching your service because of its location, hours of opening or their own physical disabilities. Some people actually prefer the greater anonymity of the telephone. The physical location of a community information service whose work is mainly or entirely conducted on the telephone is less important. Staff can be occupied with other work in between calls and do not have to be tied to an enquiry desk; thus it may be possible to offer longer hours. With the additional use of an answerphone, a service could offer a 24-hour, seven-days-a-week service. A conference-phone facility enables three-way link-ups to be made and clients can be put in direct contact with a service that can help them. If in order to answer enquiries you need to move away from the telephone or for periods of time it has to be left unstaffed, then you may need to consider the convenience of a cordless phone.

However, telephones are still by no means universally available in Britain and public call-boxes are frequently inconvenient because of location, continual use or lack of privacy. Some people are deterred from using telephones because they experience difficulties in expressing themselves via this medium or the cost of making calls is a financial burden. Some services have overcome the latter difficulty by offering a Freephone or 0800 number, or by a policy of ringing back the caller as soon as contact is made.

Telephones are best suited for answering enquiries that are brief, clearly stated and uncomplicated. Time does not allow for lengthy interviewing of the client over the phone, nor is it possible to pick up those non-verbal signals which often help in assessing the true need of the client. Likewise, the client cannot see you – so make your voice welcoming. Here are some tips on answering the telephone, based on an English Tourist Board booklet supplied to Tourist Information Centres, called *How can I help you?*:

- Make sure you always have a supply of pens and paper near the telephone and that the most used sources of information are readily to hand.
- Answer the telephone promptly. You may think that letting it ring and ring is a smart way of getting over the message that you are busy, but it only annoys the caller, who imagines that you are either drinking tea or having an interesting discussion about last night's television programme or football match.
- Never use 'Hello!' – it is too casual and, at this stage, the caller may be uncertain whether they have got through to the right service or not. State clearly the name of your service, your name, and offer to help, e.g. 'Exville Information Service. This is Joan Smith. Can I help you?' If you don't want to give your name straight away, it can be left to the closing remarks, such as 'If you need to ring back, my name is Joan Smith. Thank you for calling.'
- If the caller gives their name, always use it.
- Do not smoke, eat, or drink when speaking on the phone, and definitely not all at the same time, as it impedes your speech.
- Jot down the details of the query as it is given and confirm with the caller the essence of their enquiry before answering.
- If you have to ask the caller to wait or need to leave the telephone to look up information, explain what is happening, how long you might be and, when returning, thank the caller for waiting.

● If it is obvious from the start or after an initial search that the query may take some time to answer, offer to ring the caller back – *not* forgetting to take down their telephone number and name (if you haven't got it already). If the enquirer is ringing from a public call-box, either ask them to phone back later (try to specify a time or length of time) or take down name and address and post the reply.

● When answering an enquiry by telephone, ask the caller to read back any crucial information such as amounts of money, telephone numbers, etc. as a check that they have been taken down correctly.

● At the end of the enquiry, thank the person for calling. Be positive even if the reply is negative. It's better to say 'Sorry, we haven't been able to help you on this occasion but thank you for calling and please get in touch again if you have any other queries' than 'Sorry, can't help you' – click.

A very useful adjunct to the telephone is a fax machine which will enable you to transmit and receive documents to and from other information services.

By post

Requests for information by post do not as a rule figure prominently in the work of a community information service, but they are just as important. There is a temptation to assume that postal enquiries are less urgent than the client who is breathing down your neck or hanging on the end of a telephone, and so can be dealt with whenever there is a spare moment – in other words, never! However, every enquiry is important to the person making it and should be dealt with expeditiously.

A fairly common type of postal enquiry from individuals, organizations and commercial concerns is for lists of clubs and societies on a particular topic or in a particular area. It is obviously an advantage if you have a filing system or a computer database which enables you to print out a section on request. An alternative for frequently requested information is to have it pre-printed as a list, broadsheet or leaflet (see also pp. 97–101).

Where a postal request is likely to take a little time in being answered, send off a pre-printed acknowledgement slip on receipt of the enquiry, saying something like: 'Thank you for your enquiry, which is receiving our attention. We will send you a reply as soon as possible.'

By display

People have an innate tendency to browse, picking up information in a casual fashion. An information service can take advantage of this by providing well-sited, attractive and interesting displays for putting over information to clients and passers-by. There are four main aspects of display: noticeboards; thematic displays; window displays; and outside display.

1 *Noticeboards.* A great deal of information is available in poster or broadsheet format. Some of it is free, some will come unsolicited and there are a few posters for which you have to pay. There are basically four types of poster:

- the *event* poster gives details of something that is to take place at a particular time;
- the *service* poster gives details of a service that is available – its opening hours, location, who is eligible, how to contact, etc. – and is not, as a rule, restricted to a finite date;
- the *information* poster presents hard information in an encapsulated form – benefit rates, changes in legislation, health education, eligibility for grants, etc.;
- the *persuasive* poster seeks to sell a product, change opinions, or enlist sympathies.

The displaying of posters is an activity that can frequently arouse great passion, particularly those posters concerned with moral, political or religious issues on which strong opposing views are held. This applies not only to campaigning posters but also to ones presenting straightforward information, such as an event or hours of opening of a service, e.g. family planning clinic. You need also to be sensitive to the location of a poster. A poster showing how to fit a condom may be appropriate for display in a youth information centre but not on a board just outside the children's library. Ideally, a community information service or its parent organization should draw up guidelines on what is or is not allowed to be displayed. Try to avoid the overly simplistic approach of displaying either everything or nothing at all. An 'open door' policy may, in theory, sound fine but in practice it can throw up just as many problems, such as your right to refuse to display a poster which may not be in the public interest but does not necessarily contravene the law. It has been usual to rule out commercial advertising posters, although some services now accept these but make a charge in order to raise money for the service.

There is more to displaying posters or other notices than simply sticking in a few pins. The following are a few points you might find useful:

- You can never (or rarely) have enough noticeboard space, so in planning your service – think BIG!
- If you have several boards, categorize them: coming events, sources of help, places to visit, official notices, etc.
- Don't overcrowd your noticeboards – posters should never be overlapping and obscuring each other. If you have only a limited space, change the posters regularly to give each one a chance.
- Arrange posters to look attractive – contrast posters of different shapes or colours to add interest. Move long-term posters around from time to time to give the impression of change.
- Check noticeboards regularly to ensure that out-of-date posters are not left on display and long-term posters have not become faded or tatty.

2 *Thematic displays.* Displays devoted to a particular topic or theme, if well produced, can be a useful way of drawing attention to information that is available. The theme may (a) concern a problem area identified from an analysis of enquiries; (b) relate to a current change in legislation or benefit rates; (c) be aimed at improving public awareness of an issue of current concern; (d) draw attention to benefits, grants, services or rights of which your clientele may not be aware; (e) canvass support for a cause; or (f) educate your clientele on personal matters, e.g. health, finance, etc.

Use noticeboards or – better still – free-standing boards to mount displays. There is some skill required in preparing materials and mounting an effective and attractive display. Identify someone in your organization who has a flair for this kind of work and is willing to help.

There are a number of organizations and government departments which have displays that can be borrowed free of charge or with carriage paid one way.

3 *Window display*. If your information centre is blessed with large windows looking onto a thoroughfare, then they can be used to good effect in giving out information not only to users of your service but also to casual passers-by. Displays such as those described in the section above, placed in the window, enable the information to reach beyond your own clientele and may even attract use of the service. An external window can also be used for displaying essential information when your service is closed, such as addresses and telephone numbers of emergency services, hotel or bed-and-breakfast accommodation. A number of commercial organizations have produced microcomputer-driven information points which usually stand in a window and feature local information and advertising. The computer either scrolls pages automatically or is controlled by means of touch terminals mounted on the outside of the window.

Windows or glass entrance doors may be also be used to display small ads and job vacancies. Small ads may seem trivial but they do fill an important information need in most communities and also have an added bonus of attracting people to look in your window and, perhaps, thereby become more aware of the service and of what it can offer. Small ads can also be a useful source of income for your service but, in setting up such a service, be sensitive to other small ads services in the immediate vicinity.

A job vacancies board is a much appreciated service, particularly at times of high unemployment and where your service is located some distance from the nearest Jobcentre. Either contact local firms, businesses, shops, etc. and ask if they would be prepared to display their job vacancies in your window – you might even make a charge and earn a bit of income for the service – or contact your local Jobcentre who may be prepared to let you have job vacancy cards on a regular basis. If you can afford to do so, offer to contact the firm or Jobcentre on behalf of any client who is interested in a particular job advertised, to see if it is still vacant.

Plastic display holders for small ads or job vacancy cards can be obtained from Huggle & Co. Ltd, PO Box 38, Rue-des-Pres Trading Estate, Jersey, Channel Islands.

4 *Outside display*. As well as displaying information in your own centre, consider the possibilities of display in other buildings. Many organizations, such as libraries, community centres, clinics, schools, local government offices, etc., whose doors are open to the public, are often prepared to accept the kind of window displays referred to

in section 3 above. It may be possible to circulate such displays around a number of centres and thus reach a much wider audience. Some commercial businesses, like banks and building societies, who rarely have anything interesting to show in their windows, encourage organizations to use these for displays.

With displays located on other people's premises, you will have to accept their right to reject all or part of your display if it is objectionable to them or not produced to a high enough standard. Find out first if the organization or business has a policy on what can or cannot be displayed and whether they have their own display equipment which you can use. For outside displays, other than simply posters pinned to a wall, you will need spare display boards that can be released for a length of time and the means of transporting them. The display should be checked regularly to maintain stocks of any give-away leaflets, etc., to ensure the currency of the information, and to keep it in good repair.

Another possible outlet for information is community notice-boards, which are usually located in prominent positions such as market squares, shopping malls, etc. They are most likely to be owned by the local council but it is not unknown for councils to assign the running of them to a local information centre. The sort of information best suited for this type of board is directional (map of village, town or neighbourhood and street index), showing places of interest and sources of help or coming events.

Selective dissemination of information (SDI)

This is a rather forbidding term to describe a process for transmitting information which many information services adopt quite naturally without ever having heard of the phrase. It simply means taking note of the subject interests of particular individuals or groups who use your service and supplying them with new information on their areas of interest as it becomes available. 'Taking note' can be a fairly organized and formal system involving the sending out of a questionnaire initially to discover users' interests and maintaining a card or computer file (usually arranged by subject) of those interests. However, more often than not, it is an informal system stored in the information worker's head ('I know Joe Bloggs is interested in this, I'll send him a copy'). Good information workers can even anticipate the interests of their clientele. SDI is most often used by services whose clientele are a closed group – a voluntary organization, for example – rather than ones who serve the general public. Where generalist services operate SDI, it will usually be for other information and advice workers, community workers, professionals or groups.

An SDI service can include regular scanning of new publications, journals, newspapers, press releases, annual reports, product literature and other ephemeral material or it may be rather unsystematic and random. Either way, it is a useful service, particularly for those individuals, organizations and groups who need a supply of new information in their area of interest but do not have the time, resources or expertise to search it out. It is an excellent way to win friends for your information service who in turn may be able to help you on other occasions.

Deposit files and collections

One solution to the problem of having one fixed location from which to give out information is to duplicate your information file or database and make it available to other centres. This would make it more accessible to a wider clientele but has the disadvantages that (i) you need to have a mechanism for keeping these files or databases up to date, especially if you have to rely on someone else to do the updating, and (ii) staff, where they exist, need to be trained in using the file or database so that they can help clients.

Files using loose-leaf binders or strip indexes are easier to duplicate than card files. Computer databases can easily be copied onto floppy disk(s) but depend on the recipient having compatible equipment. Those information services whose databases are stored on a mainframe computer may be able to offer other centres online access.

Some community information services have made available collections of books and other material for deposit in centres which have particular needs, such as youth clubs. This is quite a costly service to provide in terms of both resources and staff time in preparing the collections and keeping them up to date. With this type of service, it is desirable to have a monitoring mechanism so that the value of the collections can be appraised.

A good example of an information service that is duplicated and made widely available is that operated by NACAB. The material consists of specially prepared loose-leaf information sheets; leaflets and booklets; reference books; a comprehensive index; and other supplementary material, such as sources of leaflets and information about useful reference books. The system is updated by means of monthly packs containing amendments to the information sheets and leaflets; new information sheets and leaflets; a booklist of new publications; *Update* – a magazine which provides a comprehensive summary of changes in the law, etc.; and new editions of reference books. As the system is so comprehensive, it provides the factual resource for a wide range of advice and counselling services. However, it does require a substantial amount of staff time to update the files each month and occupies several feet of shelving or a whole four-drawer filing cabinet. For many organizations the costs may also be prohibitive: £644 (voluntary organizations), £900 statutory and commercial bodies) to set up the system, while the annual updating subscription from April 1993 is £340 (voluntary) and £566 (statutory and commercial). For those organizations who do not have this kind of money or do not need such detailed information, NACAB also produces a Basic Pack, contained in two loose-leaf binders, costing £29.50 (voluntary), £78.50 (statutory and commercial) to set up, with the annual updating subscription costing £37.00 (voluntary) and £61.50 (statutory and commercial). Further details can be obtained from NACAB, 115–123 Pentonville Road, London N1 9LZ (Tel. 071-833 2181).

If your problem is lack of space or staff time to update the hard-copy version or you need an information system that is portable, NACAB also caters for these needs with a microfiche version of the hard-copy pack. Microfiche are 6in × 4in transparent cards which contain up to 60 pages of information. The complete Information System is contained on approximately 330 fiche which fit into an A4 binder. Each month a complete new set of fiche is delivered and the update time takes less than 30 minutes. You will need a special microfiche reader which enlarges and displays the fiche on a screen so that they can be read. There are three microfiche versions available covering England and Wales, Scotland, and Northern Ireland. The costs for setting up are: England and Wales: £164.50 (voluntary), £176.25 (statutory and commercial); Scotland: £190.05 (voluntary), £268.80 (statutory and commercial); Northern Ireland: £188. Annual subscription: England and Wales: £493.50 (voluntary), £754.35 (statutory and commercial); Scotland: £861 (voluntary), £1344 (statutory and commercial); Northern Ireland: £1,200. As an option, users of the Information System on microfiche can have an Adviser Pack containing additional material on paper, including benefit posters, benefit calculation sheets, a list of amendments to all books in the Information System, a list of leaflets issued, amended or withdrawn, a list of sources of all the leaflets in the system, and the reference books list. Desktop and portable readers are also available. Further details from NACAB Microfiche Information, 1 Carrington House, 37 Upper Street, Royston, Hertfordshire SG8 9AZ.

An example of a more specialized information service is the National Council for One Parent Families *Information manual*, a looseleaf binder containing information on 20 categories, with a regular updating service. Details from NCOPF, 255 Kentish Town Road, London NW5 2LX (Tel. 071-267 1361).

Publications

These are one of the best means of making your information more accessible to a wider range of people than you could ever hope to reach through a static service point. Well-produced and attractive publications enhance the image of an information service and help to attract custom. The commitment of information to print inevitably attracts corrections, additions, etc. which enable your service to maintain an even more accurate and up-to-date database.

Producing publications of reasonable quality can be costly in terms of both time and money, depending on the system used for storing your information base and access to in-house printing facilities.

If your database is stored on computer then there are a number of options, as follows:

1 If you have a word-processing or desktop publishing package on the same computer or access to these within your organization, it may be possible to transfer the whole or sections of the database file into these packages and manipulate them to produce the required format and layout for publication; at which point there are again several choices:

● print out the publication on demand or in small quantities (assuming your computer has a printer) – not practical for lengthy documents;

● print off one copy on your computer printer and photocopy – best for short documents with a limited run where quality is not critical;

- produce printed master copy for printing in-house or by a commercial printer using offset litho – master copy needs to be produced on good quality laser or bubblejet printer; (*Tip:* You can improve the appearance of text produced on a dot matrix printer by reducing it slightly on a photocopier or, better still, asking the printer to do it photographically – don't forget to allow for this by making your document format slightly larger.)
- copy the document to a floppy disk and take it to a printer who has equipment and software compatible with yours.

2 If you don't have access to word processing or desktop publishing, you may still be able to copy your database or sections of it to a floppy disk which can be read by a commercial printer with compatible equipment. The production costs will be higher as the printer will need to format, design or lay out the publication according to your specifications.

When you are planning the computerization of your information system, it is worth ensuring that all your software packages are compatible not only on your computer but also with systems that are to be found in most printing firms nowadays. It may be worth investing a little more to get an integrated package that offers a suite of facilities – database, word processing, spreadsheet, graphics and communications service - that allows you to swap documents or bits of documents from one facility to another with ease. See Chapter Eight for more details on the use of computers in community information work.

If you have a manual database, then a lot more work is necessary to transcribe the data into a form suitable for printing. Once you are at that stage, and if you do not have in-house printing facilities, it will pay you to shop around for printers. Get at least three estimates – you may be surprised at the variations in both price and the size of the publication (if this has not already been determined). Ask to see examples of the printer's work so that you can get an idea of quality. If you have a limited budget, look out for community printers or resource centres which offer services at virtually cost price of materials, though you may have to do much of the work yourself (with guidance). Alternatively, explore the possibilities of: (a) joint publication with other organizations; (b) obtaining a grant from an appropriate body who may have an interest in your publication; (c) sponsorship; and (d) advertising, or a combination of these.

Once information is printed, it is static and, therefore, liable to date in a short space of time. When producing a publication always consider your ability to sustain not only one issue but also any future new editions which may be necessary, to distribute copies, either as a one-off or regularly, or to handle sales. All these can be very time-consuming. It is an acceptable strategy, of course, to publish one issue in the hopes that its value will be recognized and future issues will attract funding. The frequency with which you need to update the publication should determine the format you choose – whether it should be loose-leaf or not, a leaflet or a booklet.

Publications may be aimed at basically two kinds of user: those whose work or status consists wholly or in part in informing others and those whom we might term your general clientele. They may be the public, a section of the public, or members of a particular organization or group. The major differences between the two in respect of publications will lie in the degree of detail and the way the information is presented.

How do you know what to publish?
- The kind of enquiries your community information receives will be one indicator. Frequent requests for the same type of information, e.g. addresses of playgroups, could be answered more quickly if a printed list or leaflet is available to give away.
- Identification of a gap in the coverage of a topic as a result of analysing enquiries or seeking information.
- Recent development or change which has not yet spawned any interpretative literature.
- Local issues.
- Discussions with other information and advice workers.
- Identification of specific groups who have defined information needs, e.g. elderly or disabled people, parents with children under five, school leavers, or the unemployed, which might be met with a suitable publication.

Types of publication

Lists
These are the simplest forms of publication to compile, often arising out of repeated requests for the same kind of information. A list can

be just a single side of paper or several sheets stapled together. The arrangement is usually straight alphabetical or alphabetical under subject or place headings, depending on the topic. Lists are given out in response to an enquiry, so do not require a great deal of creative design in their production. The use of an attractive pre-printed headed paper with the logo of your service, if you have one, its address, telephone and fax numbers, can make a humble list a little more attractive and helps to publicize the service (see Figure 14). Small numbers of lists can be run off on a photocopier or, where you have a computerized database, printed out on demand; for longer runs use a stencil duplicator or an offset litho printer. If you do not have print facilities yourself, most towns of any size nowadays usually have at least one instant-print shop where good-quality copies can be obtained at a fairly reasonable price and quickly.

Leaflets

A leaflet in one respect is a kind of extrovert list; it goes out of its way to attract attention – and thus encourage people to pick it up – through design and format. This is the *information* type of leaflet, the contents of which may be much the same as a list. The two other main types are the *educational* leaflet, the objective of which is to increase understanding or awareness of a particular subject, and the *campaigning* leaflet, which sets out either to convert someone from one point of view to another, to gain sympathy and support for a cause, or to change a certain state of affairs for the better.

Thousands of leaflets are produced each year by all kinds of organizations. The quality of these leaflets varies from the extremely glossy and eye-catching to the cheap and nasty. If you are going to enter this arena, then it is important to give as much attention as possible to the design of your leaflets as to their contents, since they will have to compete for attention with commercially designed products. However, you do not have to be an artist or designer to be able to produce an attractive leaflet. Look around at examples of commercially produced leaflets for inspiration. Advertising can also be a source of abundant 'free' or non-attributable art to illustrate and add impact to your own leaflets. Other sources of material might include old engravings (particularly of the Victorian era), drawings of the great masters (Leonardo da Vinci, Dürer, Michelangelo, etc.) and instant art books (see Figure 15).

Camden Community Information Network Directory and Exchange

SECONDARY SCHOOLS IN CAMDEN

A list of Camden Local Education Authority schools taken from the Camden Community Information Database - February 1992.

All entries are dated to show the month and year the information was checked.

ACLAND BURGHLEY SCHOOL
Burghley Rd   05-90
NW5 1UJ   Tel: 071-485 8515/6
Head: Mr Philip O'Hear. Local authority county secondary
school with 907 places for boys and girls from 11-19 with
140 in the 6th form. Part of the LA SWAP 6th form
consortium.

CAMDEN SCHOOL FOR GIRLS
Sandall Rd   09-90
NW5 2DB   Tel: 071-485 3414
Head Teacher Mr G. Fallows. Voluntary aided (Frances Mary
Buss Foundation) comprehensive girls' school with 723
places, age range 11-19. Boys admitted to the 6th form
from 1990.

HAMPSTEAD SCHOOL
Westbere Rd   09-90
NW2 3RT   Tel: 071-794 8133/6
Head Teacher Mrs Tamsyn Imison. Local authority mixed
county secondary school with 1180 places for boys and
girls 11-18.

HAVERSTOCK SCHOOL
Crogsland Rd   09-90
NW1 2BJ   Tel: 071-267 0975
Head Teacher Janet Wallace. Local authority
co-educational county secondary school with 900 places
for boys and girls 11-18.

J.F.S. SCHOOL
175 Camden Rd   09-90
NW1 9HD   Tel: 071-485 9416
Head: Mrs Jo Wagerman. Voluntary aided secondary
school with places for 1366 pupils 11-19; 55% girls, 45%
boys.

**LA SAINTE UNION ROMAN CATHOLIC CONVENT
SCHOOL**
Croftdown Rd   05-90
NW5 1HD   Tel: 071-485 5414/5
Head: Sister Theresa Finn. Girls' voluntary aided
Catholic comprehensive school with 900 places for girls
11-18. Sixth form of 160 students. Part of LA SWAP Sixth
Form Consortium.

MARIA FIDELIS ROMAN CATHOLIC SCHOOL
34 Phoenix Rd   10-91
NW1 1TA   Tel: 071-387 3856
Headteacher Sister Jo Grainger. Lower School at North
Gower St, NW1 Tel: 071-387 2359. Voluntary aided
comprehensive secondary girls' school with 900 places for
girls 11-19 and boys in the 6th form.

PARLIAMENT HILL SCHOOL
Highgate Rd   09-90
NW5 1RL   Tel: 071-485 7077
Headteacher Mrs J. Bax. Local authority county secondary
girls' school with 972 places. Part of the LA SWAP 6th
form consortium.

SAINT RICHARD OF CHICHESTER SCHOOL
Royal College St   09-90
NW1 9LY   Tel: 071-485 4593/6881/3561
Head: Miss M. Philpott. Roman Catholic voluntary aided
secondary mixed school with 600 places for boys and girls
11-19. Annexe in Prince of Wales Rd, NW5.

**SOUTH CAMDEN COMMUNITY SCHOOL (Formerly SIR
WILLIAM COLLINS SCHOOL)**
Charrington St   09-90
NW1 1RG   Tel: 071-387 0126
Also at the Ina Chaplin Centre, Sir Christopher Hatton
Building, Rosebery Ave, EC1. Headteacher: Mr H.
Salisbury. Local authority mixed county secondary school
with places for 750 boys and girls 11-19.

WILLIAM ELLIS SCHOOL
Highgate Rd   12-91
NW5 1RN   Tel: 071-267 9346
Head: Mr M.W. Wheale. Voluntary aided secondary school
with places for 800 boys 11-19. Joint 6th form at
Parliament Hill Girls' School.

Community Information Services, 100 Euston Rd, NW1 2AJ

Fig. 14 *Secondary schools in Camden*, **Camden Community Information
Network Directory and Exchange (Cindex), 1992.**

Fig. 15 *HELP: information on everyday problems for individuals and groups* (Cambridgeshire Libraries & Information Service), showing use of an instant art graphic.

If you have access to a computer, the possibility is opened up to you of investing in a graphics package which enables you to draw and design your own artwork or to buy in copyright-free art files that can be manipulated for your own purposes.

Lettering in a wide variety of styles which can be rubbed onto artwork is available in large and small sheets from most stationers, or your organization may well have invested in a lettering machine. Use cartoons, diagrams, graphs and photographs to liven up the text. Keep wording simple and short. Standard sizes of leaflets are A5 (149mm × 210mm) and 1/3A4, but experiment with unusual sizes based on standard sheets for added impact. Have enough copies printed to give a wide circulation and distribute them through as many outlets as possible, particularly those which attract large numbers of people. If the leaflet is aimed at a particular group in the community, identify specific ways of reaching them. Investigate other means of distribution that might give you an even wider coverage, such as insertion in a free community newspaper, with the council rates demand, or through organizations which regularly send out to a large mailing list.

Posters
The aim of a poster is to present a small amount of information with the maximum amount of impact so that 'he who runs may read'. Use posters to advertise events or your service, to draw attention to a few sources of information and advice, or to point out eligibility for a service or benefit. Much of the advice given above about the design of leaflets applies equally to designing posters. The design of a poster should emphasize and complement the information that you want to convey. Remember that some of the most successful posters contain no words at all. Let the image do the talking.

Don't make the poster too big as this may create problems for those whom you might wish to display it, since most organizations do not have unlimited display space. A3 (297mm × 420mm) is the most popular and useful size; A4 (210mm × 297mm) is a little small to make a great deal of impact but may be more acceptable if you want organizations to display the poster for a long time. Ideally, you should produce posters in a variety of sizes to suit varying locations.

A one-off poster can be prepared by hand if you have someone artistically inclined, but for any quantity you will need to have access to printing facilities or a good photocopier capable of enlarging and reducing. Use coloured copier paper for effect if you are printing only in black. Colour photocopiers are becoming more widely available but copies are considerably more expensive and may only work out cheaper than printing for very short runs. Another method of reproduction for posters is silk screen, which is a kind of stencil process. Some community arts centres make silk-screen facilities available to groups and will show you how to go about it.

See pp. 117, 127–8 for a list of books giving useful tips on producing leaflets and posters.

Directories

A directory is one of the most useful publications that a community information service can produce. It may cover the whole of a community, be confined to the interests of a particular client group, or contain information about a certain type of organization, e.g. social welfare agencies, local government services, etc. A directory plays an important role in community development by informing people about the services that exist and thus encouraging them to take a more active part in community life. It helps newcomers fit into the community and is a tool for those people to whom others turn for help and advice.

A directory will usually be based on an information service's database but reproduced in a format that is easy to understand and use. There are a number of decisions to make before you embark on producing a directory, regarding such as the following:

1 *Who is it aimed at?* The general public (i.e. all households), sections of the public with special needs, community groups, community leaders, etc.

2 *How many copies will be required?* This will depend on whether you decide to distribute to everyone, in which case you need to obtain an estimate of your target group. If it is not feasible to give it such a wide distribution, then you must decide on how many copies it is realistically possible to produce within your budget.

3 *How much will it cost?* You will need to work out as accurately as possible what size the directory will be so that estimates can be obtained from printers. Allow for advertising space if you are using this method to finance the directory. Newspapers work on a formula of two thirds advertising to one-third editorial (information) but they have greater overheads to contend with. Half-and-half or even less

may be an acceptable proportion, depending on your advertising rates and whether the advertising is intended to cover the whole cost.

4 *How is it to be funded?* From your own budget? By special allocation from a parent body? Joint funding with other agencies? Grants from outside bodies? Sponsorship? Advertising? Sales? Or a combination of several of these? Local newspapers often take a strong interest in producing directories of their communities. These are generally paid for by advertising and are distributed free of charge either as a pull-out supplement or as an integral part of a particular issue of the newspaper. It may be worth pursuing this alternative at the outset as it could save your information service much time and expense, and ensure that the information is made widely available.

5 *What format?* This will depend to a certain extent on the number of copies to be produced and the target group. A directory aimed at the whole of a community and containing a lot of information will need to be produced as a book, rather like a telephone directory. An alternative is to publish it as a supplement to a newspaper, but this carries the danger that it will be discarded with the newspaper and not kept for reference. If you intend to produce just a small number for use by other information centres and agencies who have contact with the public, then a loose-leaf format may be more appropriate, since it allows you to send out updated sheets as information changes. Consider any special needs of your target group, e.g.. elderly people will require larger type, people with disabilities will require a format that can be handled easily.

6 *How is it to be distributed?* Delivered free to all households? Supplement in local newspaper? Insert in a community newspaper? On request or sold at certain specified centres? Through individuals who have contact with the public or target group, e.g. social workers, health visitors, teachers, etc.?

7 *Content and arrangement* It is not possible here to go into detail about the scope and arrangement of directories because these will vary depending on the nature of the directory, but the following guidelines may be of help:

● *Scope*. This should be clearly defined before you start. Decide the geographical area to be covered and the topics included. The majority of space will be taken up with entries for organizations, clubs, societies, agencies, services, etc. but some directories may include a certain amount of 'hard' information, even if this is simply a profile of the area. There is a thin line between what constitutes a directory and what a handbook (see the section below).

● *Detail of entries.* This will depend on the directory's target group. If you are producing it for use by other information agencies or community workers, then you may need to provide the full range of information collected for your database (see pp. 63–4), as those using the directory will need as much information as possible in order to assess the usefulness of an organization to their clients. For general use, it is best not to give too much information as this may result in confusion and render the directory too cumbersome for efficient use. The minimum amount of information for each entry should give the name of the organization, persons to contact, address and/or telephone number, and a brief description of the aims of the organization where this is not self-evident from the name. The examples listed here (Figures 16 and 17) show a full and a short directory entry.

YOUR PLACE

Young People's Information and Action Centre
2 The High Street, Middletown: Tel. 519

Contact name: Jill Smith

Mon, Wed, Fri	10am - 3pm
Tues, Thurs	6pm - 9pm

No appointment necessary

Primarily intended for young people aged 11-18 and living within the Middletown area.

Services provided:

Information:	all subjects
advice and practical assistance:	housing, employment, financial and welfare rights
specialist adviser:	qualified solicitor available (Tues 6pm - 8pm, appointment necessary)
special services:	representation given or arranged at housing and welfare rights tribunals

---

Fig. 16 Full directory entry (from *Who knows? Guidelines for a review of local advice and information services and how to publicise them them*, National Consumer Council, 1982, p.17).

104

Black and Ethnic Minorities

Bengali Workers' Action Group
I Robert Street, NWI 3JU
☎ 071-388 7313

Camden Chinese Community Centre
173 Arlington Road, NWI 7EY
☎ 071-267 3019

Camden Cypriot Women's Centre
94 Camden Road, NWI 9EA
☎ 071-267 7194

Cypriot Advisory Service
(Theatro Technis)
26 Crowndale Road, NWI ITT
☎ 071-388 7971

Hopscotch Asian Women's Centre
Basement, St. Richard's House,
Eversholt Street, NWI IBS
☎ 071-387 8747

Camden Irish Centre
52 Camden Square, NWI 9XB
☎ 071-916 2222

Latin American Women's Rights Service
London Women's Centre,
4 Wild Court, WC2B 5AU
☎ 071-831 4145

Refugee Council
3-9 Bondway, SW8 ISJ
☎ 071-582 1162 Advice line

Somali Community Central London
Abbey Community Centre,
222c Belsize Road, NW6 4DJ
☎ 071-624 8378 Sundays only

Young People

Camden Careers Office
31 Kentish Town Road, NWI 8NN
☎ 071-485 3451

Camden Under 25s Advice Centre
2-6 Camden High Street, NWI OJH
☎ 071-388 4343

Older People

Camden Age Concern
335 Grays Inn Road, WCIX 8PX
☎ 071-837 3777

Counsel and Care - Advice and Help for Older People
Twyman House,
16 Bonny Street, NWI 9PG
☎ 071-485 1566

Parents

Maternity Alliance
15 Britannia Street, WCIX 9JN
☎ 071-837 1265
Enquiries on maternity rights
and benefits by letter or
telephone.

Emotionally Distressed People

Compass Project
309 Grays Inn Road, WCIX 8QF
☎ 071-278 3381
Deals only with Bloomsbury and
Islington Health Authority part
of Camden.

MIND in Camden
9-15 Camden Road, NWI 9LJ
☎ 071-911 0822

Disabled People

DISC (Disabled in Camden)
7 Crowndale Road, NWI ITU
☎ 071-387 1466

Network for the Handicapped
16 Princeton Street, WCIR 4BB
☎ 071-831 8031

Prisoners and Ex-prisoners

Inner London Probation Service
Camden House,
199 Arlington Road, NWI 7HA
☎ 071-267 9231
1a Frederick Street, WCIX ONG
☎ 071 -278 7733

Fig. 17 Short directory entry (from *Where to go for welfare rights advice in Camden*, London Borough of Camden, 1992).

● *Arrangement.* Directories can be arranged in a number of ways. A fairly common method is alphabetically by name of organization under broad subject groups which in turn may be further subdivided. Where the directory covers a number of distinct and separate towns or neighbourhoods, you may want the primary arrangement to be geographical. Other possibilities include one alphabetical arrangement by name of organization, with a subject index if required or an A–Z by subject (see Figure 9). A contents page at the beginning may be necessary to locate sections quickly. Also include at the beginning any information that may be required urgently, such as emergency services. Directories are used mainly to locate specific items of information quickly, so if the arrangement is not clear and well signposted, you may need to provide an alphabetical index. Certainly, in a directory aimed at other information services, there will be a need to index by the subject interests of agencies, groups, etc. as well as by their names. If there is more than one entry per page, then each entry should be given a running number to which the index should refer, rather than a page number.

There is some useful advice on preparing directories of local information in the following books:

Directory enquiries: how to produce a local guide to services for the under fives, Voluntary Organizations Liaison Council for Under Fives (VOLCUF), c/o Thomas Coram Foundation, 40 Brunswick Square, London WC1N 1AZ, 1988.

Getting the message across: designing guides to local services and making sure they get to the people who need them, National Information Forum, Charitybase, The Chandlery, 50 Westminster Bridge Road, London SE1 7QY, £3.50.

Who knows? Guidelines for a review of local advice and information services and how to publicise them, National Consumer Council, 1982.

Current awareness bulletins
Pleas for up-to-date information are often made by workers in many spheres of activity who do not have the time themselves to search the literature. Community workers, social workers, information and advice workers, doctors and health visitors are just a few of the

groups which might benefit from a regular flow of information. Current awareness bulletins are one of the best ways of supplying that information in an easily digestible form. In essence a current awareness bulletin is a duplicated listing of items of information which would be of use to a certain group or groups of workers. Such items might include the following:

● *Periodical articles.* Title, author, précis and source (periodical, volume number, date, page numbers of article).
● *New publications.* Author, title, publisher, date, price, address of supplier, and précis.
● *Other new materials.* Leaflets, posters, packs, audiovisual materials, etc. – give title, reference number, price (if any), address of supplier, explanatory note if necessary.
● *Short items of 'hard' information.* New regulations or legislation, benefit rate changes, changes of address or telephone number, new personnel, new services, successful cases, etc.
● *Press releases.* Subject, précis, source.
● *Courses.* Subject, dates, venue, price, address for applications.
● *Additions to library.* Author, title, publisher, date and filing number.

Where a publication or periodical is available locally, it is helpful to state this at the end of each item using for brevity, if necessary, some sort of code to indicate location, with a key provided at the beginning or end of the bulletin. Each item should be given a distinctive number so that requests for further information, photocopies or loan of material can be identified clearly and simply. The usual method is to use a combination of the year and a running number, e.g. 83/1, 83/2, etc. The most common way of arranging the entries in a current awareness bulletin is to group them under subject headings with a contents page at the beginning. Under each subject group arrange entries alphabetically.

Before deciding to compile your own current awareness bulletin, find out what is already produced both locally and nationally, to avoid carrying out work that is already being done elsewhere. It may be possible, with permission, to adapt an existing bulletin to your own local use. Seek help from other agencies with compiling and finance. The bulletin shown here (Figure 18) was produced jointly by an Advice Workers' Group and the public library, with finance from the local CVS. If necessary, to cover costs or postage, the bulletin

HOUSING

147/83

'Housing problems? Building
repairs, fair rents, tenancy
agreement rates. How the
Chartered Surveyors Voluntary Service can help'. Free
leaflet available from Royal
Institute of Chartered Surveyors, 12 Great George
Street, London, S.W.1.

148/83

Rent - 'Going to the Rent
Officer' by David Skinner.
Amply illustrated and
delivered in plain English, a
useful guide for tenants
wishing to go it alone.
Available from South Sheffield Inner City Community
Project, 14 Ranby Road,
Sheffield, S11 7AJ, price £2.
inc. p.&p.

149/83

'Security of tenure in the
private rented sector' by
Peter Robertson and Martin
Seaward (Association of
Housing Aid, £4.50) - manual,
written by Housing Advisers,
is intended mainly for those
giving advice to private
sector landlords and tenants.
Copies from Peter Robertson,
Brent Housing Aid Centre, 196
High Road, Willesden, NW10.
Add 95p postage & packing.

150/83

'Women and homelessness' -
report by K. Glock and others.
Useful compilation of existing
data on homeless women. Published by National Cyrenians,
available from Women and Homelessness Group, 54 Devonshire
Road, Cambridge - no price
indicated.

LEGAL

151/83

County Court fees - enforcement of a judgement - new
rates listed on form EX50B
from local County Court.

152/83

'Legal aid - financial limits
as from 1st April, 1983' - new
edition of free leaflet,
copies from address No. 3.

PERSONAL

153/83

'Gays and the law' by Paul
Crane (Pluto Press, £4.95) -
book primarily for gay men
giving thorough review of
police practice and examples
of abuse in law enforcement,
together with recommen-
dations for a gay movement
strategy to liberalise the
law. Useful advice on presenting a defence to criminal
charges.

154/83

'Personal application for probate or letters of administration' (Form PR48) - new
edition of form. Copies free
from Probate Office, Clifton
House, Broadway, Peterborough.

TRANSPORT

155/83

'Children's safety in cars' -
new leaflet describes how the
new seat belt legislation
affects children and gives
advice on carry cot re-
straints, child safety seats
and restraints and booster
cushions. Copies free from
Education Section, BSI, 2 Park
Street, London, W1A 2BS.

**Fig. 18 Current awareness bulletin (from *Advice workers' news*, Peter-
borough Council for Voluntary Service).**

can be made available on payment of a subscription. You might be able to save on postage by using another organization's distribution network, e.g. CVS, library, local government.

Handbooks

Handbooks often contain directory-type information but mainly the text comprises descriptive information, e.g. about services, rights of individuals or groups, advice on personal matters, courses of action, etc. Handbooks are usually aimed at groups of people who have particular needs – elderly people, people with disabilities, parents of children under five, young people – or they may cover a defined geographical area. You may have to get help with writing the text from people who have knowledge of the subject. The arrangement of a handbook will depend to a certain extent on its subject but a simple method is to use broad headings arranged alphabetically. A contents page and index are essential for locating specific items of information quickly. Use illustrations to break up the text and add interest (see Figure 19). Handbooks can be expensive to produce and you will probably need to get help with finance. Try local authorities,

Family Centres

ORTON FAMILY CENTRE
Orton. Family Centre Project is a community resource based in the Nursery Wing of St John's Church School and in the Project House, Riseholme, Orton Goldhay, Peterborough. It works together with parents, professionals and volunteers to provide a range of pre-school services for 0 - 5 year olds and support for parents of underfives living in the Orton area.
The Project has a well established Playgroup, Toy Library and Thrift Shop. It also provides opportunities for parents to play with their children through Parent and Toddler groups, Messy Play sessions and a Home Visiting scheme called Playvisitors.
Discussion groups, Drop-In sessions, exercise classes and courses for parents are also held weekly with a creche facility when required. The Centre acts as a resource for childminders, playgroups, self-help groups, and all underfives workers.
The Project receives Grant Aid from three main sources - Save the Children Fund, Cambridgeshire County Council and Peterborough City Council. The Governors of St John's Church School also support the Project by allowing the use of the Nursery Wing of the school and other parts of the building when

necessary. The Project is managed by representatives from the funding bodies and elected people from the local community.
Further details can be obtained by contacting the Project Leader at the Centre Tel. 236830.

Sarah C.

Fostering

What is fostering? Fostering is a way of providing family life for children, and this includes some underfives who for various reasons cannot live with their own parents whether for a short or long time. For example:
* Their mother may have to go into hospital for a short time because she is having another baby, or because she is ill.
* There may be family problems, or difficulties with jobs or housing.
* They may be handicapped children who live with foster families for a holiday or to give their own family a break.
When children are fostered it is very important for their parents to visit them so that when possible they can return home quickly. This is especially important with very young children. Many different kinds of people become foster parents, but they are all able to offer a loving and secure home. Some foster families have young children of their own; some are older couples with grown-up families; others may not have any children of their own. Some foster one child at a time; others more than one; some foster only babies and toddlers; others particularly like to foster teenagers. The Social Services Department would be pleased to hear

Fig. 19 *Underfives handbook: services in Peterborough Health District,* **Peterborough Information Group, 1988.**

area health authorities, groups who represent those covered by the handbook or local charities, like Lions, Rotary Clubs, Junior Chambers of Commerce. Alternatively you might seek sponsorship from local business or sell advertising space in the handbook.

Packs

Packs are an increasingly popular form of making information available, especially to people who perhaps do not have a habit of reading books. They are also useful for community information services that have limited staff resources and where the service offered is mainly of the self-help type. Packs vary from a simple plastic bag to specially embossed or printed folders. Their chief attraction is that they enable a number of flimsy items on a related theme such as leaflets, information sheets, small booklets, flow-charts, sample forms and letters, booklists and address lists, etc., to be brought together in such a way that the whole is greater than the sum of the parts. Sometimes it is necessary to link items with a specially prepared text. Packs are easily duplicated for distribution to outlying centres and, if well produced, can entice people to browse through them who otherwise would not use a more conventional book form. Some organizations even produce them to give away (see Figure 20).

Some disadvantages to packs are that they need to be displayed face outwards for maximum impact; they need to be regularly checked and updated (less easy the more they are dispersed); and without careful and attractive presentation they can so easily appear to be just a rag-bag of assorted ephemera.

The following guidelines may be helpful in preparing packs:

- *Choose the topic* – this might well be (i) a subject of frequent enquiry, e.g. buying and selling a house, adoption, writing a CV; (ii) a subject on which there is very little information in book form or that which exists is not readily understandable to the layperson, e.g. pensions, VAT registration; or (iii) a subject that meets the needs of a particular group, e.g. one-parent families, those with debt problems.
- *Identify* suitable material and obtain in required quantities.
- *Write or compile* any linking material, lists of addresses and further sources of information. Get help from people who have special knowledge of the subject, if necessary.

Fig. 20 *Back to work pack*, Step One Help & Advice Centre, 1992.

- *Number* items and list them on a contents sheet.
- *Design* a title sheet which can be inserted into or stuck on the pack.

Manila wallets for packs can be obtained from most stationers, usually in A4 or foolscap sizes. You may also be able to find a stationer who stocks ready-made transparent plastic folders but, if not, Celsur Plastics Ltd stock these and will make them to your specifications, if necessary (see p. 41). If your funding will stretch to it, then you might like to go in for custom-designed plastic or manila folders.

The media

Newspapers, local radio and, latterly, cable television can be important vehicles for getting information to the public, in addition to their usual fare of sensational stories. The media will often readily accept offers of free material from outside organizations, provided it is presented to them in the right way and would be of interest to their readers, listeners or viewers. The great advantage in using the media is that your information will reach a much wider audience than it ever would by any other means of dissemination, even if said means is not a very permanent one. Of course, the decision as to how that information is presented to the public will be out of your control. However, I have found that in the case of regular articles, columns or scripts, provided you have clear guidelines on what is required by the particular media in terms of length, style and content and keep to them, the material will not be altered very much.

The kinds of topic in which the media might well be interested are (i) forthcoming events, either generally or of a particular kind (e.g. sports, arts, etc.); (ii) information on new services or groups; (iii) important changes in legislation affecting people's lives; (iv) reviews of new publications; (v) general rights education; (vi) general services knowledge; (vii) information for young people (jobs, education, rights, recreation, etc.).

Think carefully about taking part in 'live' phone-in programmes on radio, if this is offered. You will not be able to bring your information service into the studio and you can lay yourself open to all kinds of trouble by giving instant advice or information over the air without being able to check its accuracy first.

There is obviously some overlap between giving out information

112

via the media and publicizing your service through the media, which is dealt with in the next chapter. Just giving out information, provided your service is credited, is a form of publicity, but I will confine myself here to just a few pointers on using the media for information giving alone:

- *Contact the media* – make sure they know about your community information service and what it can provide.
- *Find out* if there is a reporter who covers the areas of your service and get to know him or her.
- *Regularly feed* information to the media.
- *Make yourself available* for interview on topics of interest to your service, even at times you might consider inconvenient.
- *Don't be put off* by one bad experience with the media – tomorrow is another day.

Further information on using the media, including recommended reading, will be found on pp. 119–26.

I have concentrated in this chapter on the dissemination of information collected by an information service and available in its files. All the methods covered above can also be used to disseminate information about the service itself. This is *publicity* and is the subject of the next chapter.

Chapter Six

Publicity and promotion

All the methods covered in the previous chapter on disseminating information can also be used to publicize the community information service itself. Indeed, a service is frequently judged on the quality of all its output, not on publicity alone.

It is simply not enough, however, to set up an information service and expect people to come flocking to your door, however good it may be. While there will always be some persistent souls who find their way, even when you hide your light under a bushel, nevertheless, as a general rule, people need to be constantly and effectively reminded of the existence of your service and what it can offer, since it is never possible to predict the time when they might have need of it. Therefore, depending on your budget, you need to make publicity available through a variety of forms and outlets. The following are the main methods of publicizing a service and these will be considered in this chapter:

- name and logo;
- posters and leaflets;
- displays;
- the media and video;
- talks;
- advertising.

Name and logo
Opinion tends to be divided over the necessity for a community information service to have a distinctive name. I believe it is important for a service to have a name that is easily memorable and indicates something of the nature of that service. It is particularly important where the service marks a new departure for an existing

organization which may not be readily associated in people's minds with the new service offered. Some of the more successful community information services set up by libraries in the USA, Britain and Australia have had distinctive names which feature on letter headings, in articles, and across publicity of all kinds. Ideally, the name should reflect the nature of the service and does not *always* have to be an acronym. Examples from the voluntary sector include Relate (marriage guidance service), Gingerbread (single parents), DIAL (Disablement Information and Advice Line), Shelter (housing advice) and Mind (mental health).

In addition to a distinctive name, it is helpful to have a symbol or 'logo' which people can instantly recognize and which gives the service a sense of identity (Figure 21).

Fig. 21 Peterborough Information Group logo.

A useful book that may have some relevance to creating the identity of your community information service is:

Kirby, John, *Creating the library identity: a manual of design,* Gower, 1985, £39.00.

Posters and leaflets
A simple and effective means to advertise your information service is to produce posters, handbills or leaflets for display from a wide variety of outlets. These do not necessarily have to be sophisticated or expensive – some quite impressive results can be achieved using minimal resources with a bit of imagination. The books listed on pages 127–8 should give you some ideas on how to do it.

Posters are ideal for getting across small amounts of information in an eye catching way. As a rule, they should give only the name of the service, address, telephone number, hours of opening and, where necessary, any explanatory words to make it clear what kind of service is offered and to whom. To be effective a poster must catch people's attention and present the right image of your service, rather than bombard the viewer with information. There are several ways to catch attention – through typography, paper (e.g. 'day-glo' or an unusual shape or size) and graphics. Try to get your posters displayed in as many places as possible: libraries, community centres, shops, clinics, surgeries, local government offices where the public call, sports centres, schools, youth clubs, anywhere that people gather in any numbers. If possible, have the poster available in a variety of sizes. A small size is particularly useful if you want others to display them permanently.

Handbills are usually single unfolded sheets of paper, either A4 size or, more commonly, A5, printed on one or both sides. A quick and simple way to produce a handbill is to use the same design as your poster reduced in size. If necessary, the other side of the handbill can be used to give more details of your service. Handbills are best suited for placing on counters, tables or any flat or sloping surface for people to take; for handing out at exhibitions, in the street or other public places; or for inserting in community and local newspapers, magazines or other organizations' mailshots.

Leaflets are one of the most popular means of publicizing a service and differ from handbills in having one or more folds to produce several sides, of which the front normally carries an attractive design to encourage people to pick them up. As well as the basic information contained on the poster or handbill, a leaflet can also include a fuller description of your service. However, it is advisable still to keep the number of words to the absolute minimum – quality not quantity is the watchword. The leaflet should be clear, easy to read and to the point. Use illustrations or cartoons to break up the text and to give added emphasis to the words (see Figure 22). A leaflet is as much about creating an image of the service as it is about giving information. Take a leaf from commercial advertising: this often says nothing or very little about the product but tries to create a good feeling – excitement, desire, greed, even an irresistible urge – for it.

116

CONSUMER PROTECTION DEPARTMENT

Enforces consumer protection legislation, such as the Weights & Measures Act, Trade Descriptions Act, Consumer Protection Act, etc. Advises traders on their obligations under the legislation and investigates complaints from the public.

Consumer Protection Department,
St. Peter's Road,
Peterborough.
Tel: 51577

Open:
Monday – Friday   8.45 a.m. – 1.00 p.m.
                             2.00 p.m. – 5.20 p.m.
Area Controller: R. Slater

Fig. 22 Peterborough Information Group leaflet listing information and advice services in the city.

You don't have to go quite that far, but the principle is the same.

The following book can be recommended for practical advice on producing posters, handbills and leaflets:

Pyle, Jon and Harrington, Simon, *Making leaflets work: the librarian's guide to effective publicity*, Publicity and Public Relations Group of the Library Association, 1988.

Displays

In the last chapter your attention was drawn to the usefulness of displays for disseminating information to a wider audience. The same methods and outlets can also be used to promote your own service. Try to present as many aspects of your information service as possible, keeping it simple at the same time. Wording should be large and clear enough to be seen at a distance and relatively brief. Displays are essentially visual, so try to get some good photographs to illustrate your service, not ones obviously posed but rather taken informally. For a display that is intended to sell a service, the photographs should be about people, not your front door, photocopier or leaflet rack. Small photographs, however good, do not make an impact on a large display, and you would do better to spend your money on one extra large blow-up that encapsulates the essence of your service. Photographic enlargements are expensive, although some of the mail-order photographic processors do a poster-size enlargement (up to 20in × 30in) from black-and-white or colour negatives and slides for around £6.00 (1992 prices). Colour photocopiers can also produce excellent results, usually enlarging up to A3 size, at substantially less than this price.

Another way to get your service known is to have a manned exhibition or stand at large events, such as agricultural shows, trade fairs, country fairs, ideal home exhibitions, leisure fairs, markets, etc. In addition to providing a static display about your service, you might also consider running an enquiry or advice service on the spot, but be sure that you can deliver the goods, since failure will reflect badly on your service. Don't expect to get too many enquiries, however, as most people attend shows and the like to enjoy themselves and leave their problems at home. It helps to have some sort of gimmick to attract attention, like the monster jigsaw puzzle shown here (Figure 23) used by Peterborough Information Group at a local agricultural show. The same year, the group also borrowed two pigs for a competition to 'guess their weight', with the proceeds going to two local charities for disabled people.

If the cost of taking part on your own in this kind of show is too prohibitive, you might consider the possibility of sharing with other organizations or begging space on someone else's stand. You will need to allow sufficient staffing to cover the hours of the show, including meal times, and to continue your normal service. You may also need to arrange transport for display boards and equipment to and from the show and security for them while they are there.

It is always difficult to assess and virtually impossible to calculate how valuable such exercises are in attracting extra custom to a service. If they do no more than bring the service before the eyes of a

Fig. 23 Peterborough Information Group jigsaw at East of England Show.

great number of people who probably knew nothing about it before, then they may be worth while.

The media
Press, radio and television are important means of publicizing your community information service, since they offer the potential of reaching many thousands of people from all walks of life. They are also transitory media and so need to be continually fed information about your service. It is no good thinking that an advertisement placed five years ago when your service was set up, is still going to attract users! There are basically three forms that publicity about your service could take on any medium: general features about the service, news items, and advertisements or commercials.

Newspapers
These are likely to be the most common method of publicizing your service. There are four main types: the national press, local newspapers, 'free' papers paid for by advertising, and community newspapers. The latter are usually non-commercial and serve a fairly defined neighbourhood, often being delivered to every door free of charge. They are a good means of getting your service known, as advertising is cheaper than for their commercial counterparts and may even be free for a service that helps the community. Community

newspapers are likely to be more receptive to feature articles about your service and may even be prepared to let you have a regular spot.

Many local newspapers in recent years have been transformed into 'free' papers totally supported by advertising. As a rule, these are delivered free to every door in their catchment area but, since the total cost has to be met by advertising, their rates are usually high. They still carry a certain amount of news in addition to the adverts, but not very many feature articles. They may not be read as thoroughly as newspapers for which a charge is made, since there is a tendency to regard anything free as being of little value. Their chief attraction for your service is their wide distribution, which can be exploited by either placing adverts or getting news directly in the paper or using it as a means of distributing your own handbills or leaflets.

The weekly or daily local newspaper is the one with which most people will be familiar, though it is a dying breed. It contains a mixture of news, features and advertising and, next to the community newspaper, will be the most accessible. Some actually carry a column for community service adverts, which are usually free. Local newspapers are often receptive to feature articles written either by their own staff or, more often nowadays, by the organizations themselves. Write to the editor, tell him or her about your service and ask if s/he would welcome an article. It helps if you can link the article to something that is newsworthy, e.g. an anniversary, a new service, loss or reduction in grant, or increased use, particularly if the increase relates to a growing problem, e.g. debt. If you are contributing the article, then you will need to know how many words are required, whether there is room for an illustration, and the deadline. With this kind of article, it is common practice for newspapers to run it when news is slack.

But what sells newspapers more than anything else is news which, in journalistic terms, concerns some happening or event that creates conflict, hardship or danger to the community, or even a scandal; features something unusual; or displays individualism. As well as newsworthiness, newspapers also look for that magic ingredient: 'human interest'. Telling them what you do every day of the week does not constitute news, however worthy it may be. Unusual requests or happenings do, even if they are not directly related to your service.

It is highly unlikely that a local community information service will need to use the national press to publicize its services, although there may be occasions – when a service has done or is planning something unusual, controversial or spectacular – for which it might be worthwhile to interest the national press, especially if the event has wider significance. You may also attract wider publicity by involving a famous local politician or media personality, or a government minister who may see it as a platform for issuing a policy statement. In these cases you must accept that the attention will be on the personality rather than your service. However, for services with a national clientele, the national press may well be an appropriate outlet for their news. The usual approach will be by press release, of the type shown below. In some cases it may be possible to cultivate journalists with a particular interest in community services and make a direct approach. You should also consider sending your press releases to The Press Association, 85 Fleet Street, London EC4P 4BE (Tel. 071-353 7440). This is a national press agency which, if you can get them to take up your news item, will feed it to every important newsroom in the country. However, the news will need to be pretty important or dramatic.

Magazines, specialist journals and current awareness bulletins are other possible outlets for publicizing a national information service. You should by now be aware of the periodicals which cover the areas of work relating to your service but, if you need further titles, both *Willings press guide* and the *Newspaper press directory* contain lists of periodicals arranged under subject headings. One or both of these will be found at most medium to large public libraries.

Radio

The expansion of both the BBC and commercial local radio networks in recent years has meant that most major urban areas of the country and much of the rural hinterland is served by at least one and sometimes more local radio stations. Most of these stations are readily accessible to community organizations and services, probably more so than local newspapers, and will usually be pleased to broadcast announcements of events free of charge. Keep details of such announcements as brief as possible, the essentials being event, date, time, place, name of person to contact and telephone number. Send details to the radio station well in advance and, if they feel that the event is of general public interest, you may be asked to come into the studio for an interview or be interviewed over the telephone. If you possibly can, it is better to go to the studio for interviews since the sound quality will be infinitely better and there is a tendency to be indiscreet over the telephone. It will also enable you to make contact with the station staff and familiarize yourself with the studio.

You may be able to interest the radio station in doing a feature about your service and, if you are lucky, they may even let you decide the format and questions; in which case, you will need to know how long the programme is to last and whether there are to be any breaks for commercials or records. As a general rule, radio producers do not like too much unrelieved talking as listeners soon lose concentration. About 4–4½ minutes is the maximum, roughly equivalent to two pages of A4 double spaced typing.

The following are further tips on being interviewed:

- Try to find out in advance of the interview what questions you are going to be asked or what topics are going to be covered.
- Jot down on one side of a card or a piece of paper the important points you want to make, names, figures, etc. – these are easily forgotten when you are on air.
- Find out the interviewer's first name and use it when answering questions: 'I'm glad you asked that, Bob, we feel that not enough people are aware ...' It makes the interview sound less of a confrontation, oral examination or third-degree interrogation.
- Never get annoyed or flustered if an interviewer is aggressive; by remaining calm and friendly you will only show up his or her bad manners and gain the listeners' sympathy.
- Never be afraid to say 'I don't know' to a question; it is far better than inventing wrong information or blustering and you can always use the opportunity to answer a question that has not been asked: 'I don't know what the answer to that is, Rita, but there is evidence of tenants being harassed by ...'
- Will yourself to speak slowly because there is a natural tendency to talk too fast on radio. However, avoid embarrassing pauses whenever possible.
- If the programme is pre-recorded, don't be afraid to say 'Can we do that again?' when you are making a bad reply; it can always be edited out.
- Avoid sarcasm – the listener cannot see your face and so will not know whether you are joking or not.
- Put a smile in your voice.
- Never rustle papers during or at the end of an interview – it sounds like a simulated storm over the radio.

With the financial resources and the expertise, you could try producing an advertisement slot for broadcasting on commercial radio stations. You will, however, be competing with firms and businesses for the available time and the prime periods throughout the day when most people tune in. I don't know if my local radio station is typical or not, but their charges for producing a commercial at 1992 prices start at £55 and increase depending on the length, number of voices used, music, sound effects, etc. Broadcasting rates vary according to the time of day or night, the length and the number of times you want the advert broadcast. For example, a single 20-second spot can cost from £22 to £104. Your local radio station will be able to advise you on the best time to reach the particular clientele served by your information service. Producing a commercial is a skilled exercise and it is worth getting expert help from an advertising agency or the local radio station itself. Ask if they have a policy of free public service announcements.

Television

Just as local radio blossomed in the 1970s and 1980s, community television looks set to flourish in the 1990s with the extension of cable franchises. Access to television for local community information services may then become a reality. However, for the moment most national and regional television channels have programmes which give access to community groups. If you feel that your service is making a unique contribution or doing something innovative, you may be able to catch the attention of a producer.

In addition to these social action programmes, many of the commercial television stations offer the facility of public service announcements. These enable local voluntary, statutory and community organizations the opportunity to 'advertise' in short slots between programmes throughout the week. Organizations can appeal for volunteers, recruit new members to self-help groups, offer services and advice to the public, or increase awareness of or interest in the work of the organization. There is no charge for the announcements and usually help is given with producing the slot. Write to your local television company to find out if they run such a scheme.

Press releases

The customary way to notify the media about news concerning an organization or service is to issue a press release. There are some simple guidelines for presenting and writing press releases which will help to bring your news to the attention of an editor or producer and prevent it from being instantly consigned to the waste-paper basket.

Presentation
- Use A4-size headed paper, ideally specially designed with the name and logo of your service and the words 'Press Release' figuring prominently.
- Put a date at the top and, if necessary, an embargo date, i.e. a date before which the press release is not to be used.
- Don't write longhand – type it, using double line spacing, and provide generous margins so that the journalist can make notes, etc.
- Type on one side of the paper and go on to a second sheet only if absolutely necessary, in which case put the word 'more' or 'mf' ('more follows') prominently at the bottom of the page.
- Provide a simple heading at the top of the press release to indicate what it is about. It does not have to be a 'catchy' heading – that's the journalist's or sub-editor's job.
- At the end of the press release put 'Ends' separately from the final sentence.
- Always put the name and telephone number of a person or persons from whom further information can be obtained.
- Staple more than one sheet together at the top.
- If something in your press release requires further or more detailed explanation, append this as 'Notes for the Editor'.

Writing
- Every press release should answer the 'five w's': *What* is happening? *Who* is doing it? *Where* is it happening? *When* is it happening? *Why* is it happening? The answers to the first four should be contained in the first sentence wherever possible, although not necessarily in the order given here.
- The first two sentences are crucial and should contain the bare bones of your news story, so that a busy journalist can see at a glance what the release is about. You can elaborate later. This is the way that most news stories are written. It allows the editor to cut off paragraphs from the end of the copy to fit it into the final page layout without losing the gist of the story.

- Keep sentences short.
- Use active rather than passive voice. *Don't* say 'A leaflet has been issued today by Exville Information & Advice Centre ...' *Do* say 'Exville Information & Advice Centre has today launched a leaflet on housing rights ...'
- Never use jargon and spell out acronyms the first time they are used in the press release.
- Use quotes where possible – journalists love these because it sounds as though they have actually been out and interviewed someone.

Specimen press release

EXVILLE INFORMATION & ADVICE CENTRE
10 High Street
Exville
EX1 2AB
Tel. 67890

PRESS RELEASE 31 May 1992

HOUSING RIGHTS LEAFLET HELPS TENANTS

Exville Information & Advice Centre has today launched a leaflet* on housing rights for tenants living in private rented accommodation. It follows a sharp rise in enquiries to the Centre concerning harassment by landlords, lack of repairs and increased rents. The leaflet sets out in simple language what action tenants can take, including the withholding of rent, prosecution for trespass, and making a complaint to the Rent Officer.

Joe Bloggs, Chairman of Exville Tenants' Association, says: 'I welcome this leaflet as it will bring to the attention of tenants that they do not have to put up with damp walls, leaking roofs and peeling paintwork or landlords who are out to make a fast buck.'

The leaflet is available free of charge from Exville Information & Advice Centre and all libraries and community centres in the town.

ENDS

Further information contact:
Doris Smith Tel. Exville 12345 (home), 67890 (work)

*copy attached

Further reading

Callaghan, J. and Yeomans, K., *Local radio kit*, National Extension College, 1983.

Drinkwater, Jane, *Get it on ... radio and television*, Pluto Press, 1984.

Jones, Maggie, *Using the media,* 2nd edn, NCVO Publications, 1992, £5.95.

Parker, Nicola (ed.), *Charities and broadcasting: a guide to radio and television appeals*, Directory of Social Change, 1988.

User's guide to the media, Inter-varsity, 1988.

Video

Video is being increasingly used by community organizations to promote their services, in staff training or to draw attention to a social or local problem. Video equipment is relatively easy to handle and portable, video cassettes are cheap and can be used over and over again, and playback can take place in any room which has an ordinary television set. Video cameras ('camcorders') are fast becoming as common as 35mm cameras but, for producing something other than home movies, you may need a range of more expensive equipment. This can often be borrowed or hired from schools, colleges, adult evening institutes, video workshops, resource centres, community arts centres or some video shops. If you are interested in using video to promote your service, the following book may be of help:

Audio-visual guide for community groups, Community Projects Foundation, 1985.

Talks

An effective and inexpensive way to publicize your information service is by giving talks to the multifarious groups in the community who are constantly on the look-out for speakers. Although the membership of such groups may be small in number, it is an opportunity not only to tell people about the service you offer but also, in discussion and questions afterwards, to get feedback from them on their needs and the effectiveness of your service. Never underestimate the power of the grapevine – you may only be talking to a handful of senior citizens, but they have the ability to pass the word on to a much wider circle.

Keep talks as brief as possible, use simple language and, where suitable, visual aids. A touch of humour, in the right place and taste, helps to get the audience on your side. Give-aways, in the form of leaflets, booklets, information sheets, etc., are often much appreciated. If possible, invite groups to visit your premises where information resources and equipment can be demonstrated – this never fails to impress.

Advertising

It is unlikely that many information services will be able to afford this type of publicity. Poster sites are not cheap and, to be effective, the publicity will need to be handled professionally. Obviously, the best sites are where a lot of people gather or pass by, such as railway stations, bus stops and stations, shopping malls, town centres or on buses. If your service is part of a larger organization like a local government authority, then they may own poster sites of their own which you may be able to use. You could always try writing to advertising agencies or owners of poster sites to see if they would donate space for your service for the public good – you never know, your plea might fall on a sympathetic ear.

At the end of the day, whatever method of publicity you use or however much or little you spend, the best publicity is a service that is successful in meeting the needs of its clientele, for news will spread by word of mouth from satisfied users. The way to ensure that your service is achieving all that it set out to do, or to find out if it ought to be doing more, is to keep it under continual review. In Chapter Seven we shall be looking at various methods of doing this.

The following books may be useful in providing more details of the methods that can be used to publicize your service:

King, Ivan, *Promote! The handbook of public library promotions*, Public Libraries Group of the Library Association, 1989, £12.95.

Kinnell, Margaret (ed.), *Planned public relations for libraries – the PPRG handbook*, Taylor Graham, 1989, £18.00.

Lowndes, Barbara, *Getting your message across: publicity for community organisations,* National Federation of Community Organisations, 1989, £4.95.

MacIntosh, Dorothy and Alastair, *A basic PR guide*, Directory of Social Change, 1985, £7.95.

Miles, John, *Design for desktop publishing*, John Taylor Books, 1987, £14.95.

Quilliam, Susan and Stephenson, Ian Grove, *Into print – how to make desktop publishing work for you*, BBC Books, 1990, £7.99.

Quinn, Patrick, *Effective copy writing for librarians*, Publicity & Public Relations Group of the Library Association, 1992, £10.95.

Semple, Audrey, *Sell space to make money*, Directory of Social Change, 1987, £2.95.

Vaughan, Jenny, *Getting into print: an introduction to publishing*, Bedford Square Press, 1988, £4.95.

Zeitlyn, Jonathan, *Effective publicity and design: a do-it-yourself guide to getting your message across*, InterChange Books, 1987, £5.95.

Chapter Seven

How to maintain an effective service

Any community information service needs to be flexible in order to respond to the changing needs of the community it serves. Therefore, the final element – and a very important one – in planning a service is to provide a means of continually monitoring its effectiveness. You need to know whether the right information is being collected and the right clientele reached; where, if any, there are gaps in provision; and how effective is your publicity for the service.

There are several ways of monitoring a service, each with varying degrees of complexity. The method(s) you choose will depend on the amount of staff time and resources you have available. They are the following:

● statistics;
● feedback;
● surveys;
● research.

Statistics

There are very few people who would claim to like keeping statistics. At best, they are looked on as an irksome necessity, only tolerable when kept as unobtrusive as possible. Staff running a busy community information service will seldom have the time to keep detailed records of enquiries, so do try to restrict them to the absolute minimum.

The barest minimum is simply to record the number of people using the centre by noting them down on a sheet of paper, using the time-honoured 'five barred gate' method (卌) or a number tally machine or 'clicker' (Figure 24). Both these methods rely on a human agent, however, and are therefore prone to inaccuracies – through

Fig. 24 Hand tally machine.

forgetfulness, preoccupation, distraction, etc. There are now counting devices available which are triggered off by customers treading on a pressure pad placed under a carpet or by breaking an infra-red beam. This statistic will only tell you the number of people who darkened your doorstep, however; they might only have been browsing or sheltering from the rain, so an alternative is to record manually the number of people making an enquiry. Nonetheless, you will not know what subjects they enquired about, whether you were successful in finding the information, or how long it took.

You can go some way towards collecting more detail and yet not create much more work by drawing up or pre-printing record sheets. These may be related to subject or length of time or both (Figure 25). Some centres, instead of using sheets, have a bank of 'clickers', but this is only practicable if you have a small number of categories, say no more than six; otherwise it becomes too complicated to remember which 'clicker' is which.

All the above methods give only a broad indication of the number of enquiries and do not reveal any detail about their nature or the degree of success in answering them. The latter aspect might be catered for by asking staff to record details of unsuccessful enquiries

Statistical Record Form 1

FEDERATION OF
INDEPENDENT
ADVICE CENTRES

Advice worker.. Month & year..

Sheet number... Location...

Enquiry Categories	New enquiries	Ongoing enquiries
1 Benefits		
2 Debt, tax & consumer		
3 Housing		
4 Employment		
5 Immigration & Nationality		
6 Family law		
7 Miscellaneous legal		
8 Education		
9 Health		
10 Local information		
11 Miscellaneous		
12 Translation & literacy		
13 Referrals to other agencies		
14 Support / needed to talk		
TOTALS		

Fig. 25 Federation of Independent Advice Centres – simple statistical form.

only, so that they can be analysed in order to detect any weaknesses in the information base that can be rectified or any sources that have been overlooked.

A more detailed recording system, found mainly in advice and counselling centres, is the day book. In effect, this is a large diary in which details of enquiries are recorded, giving the name of the client, address, date and nature of the enquiry, action taken, further action being pursued, etc. A day book has the advantage of being easy to use and allows other information and advice workers to check on the details of an enquiry if the person calls back on another occasion. It is not so convenient for extracting statistics and, should you need to refer back to an enquiry, the chronological arrangement is not helpful – people can be notoriously vague about dates. A more satisfactory method is to enter the details on cards or pre-printed enquiry forms, one for each client. These can then be filed by the client's name, so that it is easy to refer back if some time has elapsed between visits.

The system of pre-printed enquiry forms is fairly common in information centres but is rarely used for all enquiries – usually only those that take some time or require further search after the enquirer has left the centre or hung up the phone. The kinds of information that you may want to collect about each enquiry can include the following:

- *Client* – name, address, telephone number (if needed for follow-up), sex, age range, ethnic origin.
- *Enquiry* – simple précis of subject.
- *Duration* – how long it took to answer the enquiry.
- *Sources used or tried in answering the enquiry* – useful if a search is continued over a length of time to avoid duplication of effort.
- *How enquiry was received* – walk-in, telephone, post, fax.
- *Time* – will indicate spread of enquiries throughout the day.
- *How client heard of service* – may help to measure success of publicity.
- *Client's area of residence* (if address not taken) – will show from which areas most use comes and those not being reached.

Forms have the advantage that they can easily be stored for future reference and abstracting of statistics. With a subject heading or classification number added, they can become a subject file to be referred to when information on the same subject or statistics are required. In a very busy information centre, however, it is unlikely that staff will have time to fill in a form with this amount of detail for each enquiry, so you may need to consider a combination of (a) forms for lengthier enquiries and those needing to be followed up, and (b) a tally system under broad categories for quick enquiries.

The record sheet shown here (Figure 26) is a kind of compromise hybrid that was used for recording enquiries in a public library community information centre shared with other agencies on a ses-

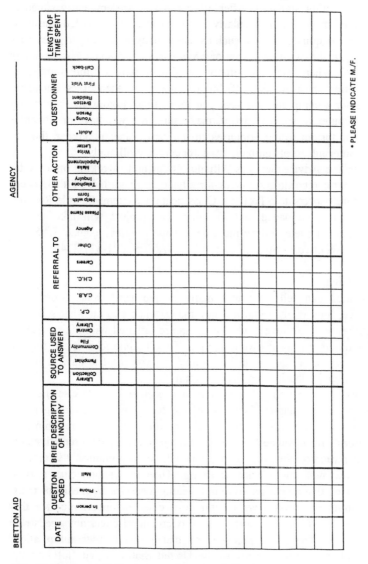

Fig. 26 Bretton Aid Centre enquiry record sheet.

sional basis. Each agency had its own pad of forms which were self-carbonated to produce an additional copy for the librarian to extract statistics.

If you have invested in a computer, there is the temptation to use it for collecting statistics. After all, computers are eminently suited to number crunching, particularly if you need to ask detailed questions of your enquiry statistics, such as 'How many women aged over sixty living in the Westward area of Exville enquired about bus passes in 1991?' Where you are simply keeping a tally of the number of enquiries in a number of broad categories, then it is debatable whether a computer will save you much time. Before you start using a computer to store statistics, make sure that you have an effective system for recording enquiries in the first place; otherwise the old computer adage of 'garbage in, garbage out' will apply.

London Advice Services Alliance is currently working on a model system for recording statistics for advice work, called STATS. There are four aspects to STATS: a Classification System, Sample Recording Forms, Guidance and Training. The project will take several years to complete and for more details and progress, contact LASA at 88–94 Wentworth Street, London E1 7SA (Tel. 071-377 2748).

Feedback

Statistics can tell you how many people used your information service, how many enquiries they made, when and on what subjects, but they will not reveal whether users are satisfied with the service or why others do not use your service. To get some idea of the impact your service is making on its community, you need to have a means of getting feedback from that community.

Two ways of doing this have already been referred to elsewhere in this book. In Chapter Two, one of the functions of the management committee was identified as to 'monitor use and recommend changes'. If, as suggested, this committee includes representatives of the community, then their comments will be very important in assessing how well the service is doing. Then in Chapter Six, it was suggested that a spin-off from publicizing a service by means of talks to community groups was that it also gave an opportunity for the speaker to ask for reactions to the service and discover any needs not being met. There is a practice, associated mainly with information and referral (I&R) centres in the United States, called 'follow-up', which is used to check on user satisfaction with the service or services to which they have been referred. At the time of the enquiry, details of the client's name and telephone number, the query and the service(s) to which referred are noted down. Then, at a later date, the client is rung back to find out if the information given was satisfactory or whether further help is required. Any adverse comments about the I&R centre are noted, so that improvements can be made. Comments about other services are noted down on the back of the appropriate card for that service in the information file. In this way, clients are encouraged to feel that they are a part of the information service and can contribute to the continual evaluation of its information files. However, follow-up is a time-consuming and costly exercise which may well be beyond the means of most community information services except on an occasional and very selective basis.

You may be able to get some useful feedback by consulting other information and advice services or community leaders in your area. They may have had comments made to them about your service and be prepared to divulge them with frankness.

Surveys
A more formal and systematic way to obtain feedback is to conduct a user survey or a general survey of your community. You do not have to be an experienced researcher to carry out a survey, provided you exercise a degree of commonsense and care in drafting or asking questions. Some elementary points to look out for in conducting a survey were discussed in Chapter One (pp. 5–8) and are worth repeating here.

Before you conduct a survey, you must have a clear idea of what you want to find out and the use to which that information is going to be put. You may only want to gather information about the existing clientele of your service, in which case a user survey is called for. On the other hand, it may be important to find out what impact your service is making on the community as a whole; therefore, the scope of the survey needs to be wider and to be conducted outside the information centre.

There are basically two methods of conducting a survey, by questionnaire and by interview. A questionnaire survey of users is the easiest to carry out as, once the form has been drafted and printed, there is little staff involvement until the analysis stage. Questionnaires can be either left on the counter for clients to take or handed to clients when an enquiry is made. The following are points to look out for:

- Number forms so that you know how many have been issued and can calculate the percentage returned.
- Make sure there is an address for returning the form and a closing date – you do not necessarily have to keep to the closing date but it helps to encourage people to return them.
- Have an open question on the form to invite any other comments about the service – this often evokes the best replies.
- Arrange a system for return of forms that has a degree of anonymity (e.g. a posting box in the centre).

With this kind of survey, it is usual to find that responses tend to be biased towards the favourable, so you will have to allow for this when interpreting results.

The other method of surveying users is by interview. This has the advantages that it is possible for the interviewer to probe for greater depth in responses, to record qualified replies to questions where the interviewee has difficulty in giving a straight yes/no response, and the interviewee can ask for clarification of any questions on which they are not sure. A disadvantage of this method, of course, is that the more non-standardized the replies, the more difficult they are to analyse and represent statistically.

You will need space in your centre to conduct interviews and staff time, although it may be possible to enlist outside help with this in the shape of volunteers or students on placement. It is unlikely that you will be able to interview every user, so an agreed proportion must be determined beforehand, say every other one or every tenth. Whatever the proportion, you will probably need two interviewers, as it is not possible for one person to interview and keep an eye on the numbers using the service in order to catch the next one. With more than one interviewer it becomes necessary to ensure that questions are posed in the same way, especially when there is a need to prompt interviewees, and that means some form of training or briefing beforehand. The remarks above about allowing for favourable bias in interpreting replies also applies here, possibly to an even greater extent, since clients are unlikely to be outwardly critical of a service when being interviewed on its premises.

A survey of the wider community needs to be drafted more carefully. Where possible, try to disguise the purpose of the survey and avoid asking leading questions ('Don't you think it's a good idea to ...') as these may colour responses. It is unlikely with both questionnaires and interviews that you will be aiming for total coverage of the community, so decide on a representative sample.

There are several possible ways of distributing questionnaires, the least satisfactory being to leave copies in public buildings (community centres, libraries, council offices, shops, clinics, etc.) for people to take. This is somewhat haphazard and may not result in a representative sample. A better alternative is to deliver by hand to every tenth house (or whatever proportion you have decided), using your own staff or volunteers. There may, however, be a simpler way of distributing by, for example, inserting copies in the appropriate proportion of community newspapers (where they exist) that are delivered to each household. You might investigate the possibility of printing the survey as part of the community newspaper. Where you can afford it, include a post-paid, addressed envelope for reply; otherwise, arrange for them to be left at suitable locations in the community.

Figure 27 is an example of a survey questionnaire aimed at finding out the use made of a library community information centre.

Interviewing of the wider community to determine use is unlikely to be a practical proposition for an information centre to conduct on its own. It is more likely to be used where an outside organization is conducting a research project on your service.

Research

Surveys are one form of research, of which there are a number of other types – operational research, action research, experimental research - most of which require a certain amount of expertise and, therefore, will need to be conducted by an outside agency, e.g. The British Library, a library school, or a university department. Interest in your information service as a subject of research will depend on whether it has innovative features or whether the aspect to be investigated is symptomatic of other information centres and thus the research findings would have a wide applicability. For a more detailed discussion of research objectives and techniques, there is an excellent guide by Nick Moore called *How to do research*, 2nd edn, Library Association, 1987.

5. HAVE YOU USED ANY OF THESE SERVICES IN PETERBOROUGH, IN THE LAST 6 MONTHS?

CITIZENS ADVICE BUREAU	
JOB CENTRE	
CONSUMER ADVICE SHOP	
TOWN HALL INFORMATION DESK	

_____

_____

_____

_____

ANY OTHER, PLEASE STATE

_____

_____

6. DO YOU USE THE CRESSET?

YES		GO TO Q7
NO		GO TO Q8

7. FOR WHAT REASON?

SHOPPING	
SPORT	
TO GO TO A DAY CENTRE	
OTHER LEISURE ACTIVITIES	

8. DO YOU USE ANY OTHER COMMUNITY CENTRE IN BRETTON?

YES	
NO	

IF SO, WHICH ONE?_____

9. WHAT OTHER ACTIVITIES SHOULD THE LIBRARY PROMOTE, AS WELL AS LENDING BOOKS AND GIVING INFORMATION.

TALKS	
EXHIBITIONS	
LEAFLETS TO TAKE AWAY	
LOANS OF POSTERS & SLIDES	
OTHER AGENCIES GIVING ADVICE IN THE LIBRARY	

THANK YOU FOR YOUR HELP.

Fig. 27 Part of a library survey conducted in Bretton Township, Peterborough, by the Public Libraries Research Unit of Leeds Polytechnic School of Librarianship.

Continuous evaluation using one or several of the techniques outlined above is essential in order to keep the service relevant to its community. By indicating strengths and weaknesses, areas of unmet need and duplication of services, it can point the way to future development of the information service. An information service needs to be a growing organism because communities do not stand still but are constantly changing, some more rapidly than others. At the beginning of this book, I stressed the need to involve the community in the planning of your information service and that is my message at the end. A community information service exists to serve its community and, therefore, the community needs to be involved at all stages. There is no guarantee, in these hard times, that your service will survive, but it stands a much better chance of succeeding and developing if it can be shown that it is respected, valued and used by the community and is performing a worthwhile function.

Further reading

Evaluation and monitoring in voluntary organisations (Reading List No. 5), NCVO Publications, 1990, £1.50.

Feek, W., *Working effectively: a guide to evaluation techniques,* Bedford Square Press, 1988, £4.95.

Lawrie, Alan, *Quality of service: measuring performance for voluntary organizations,* The Directory of Social Change, 1992, £8.95.

Chapter Eight

Using computers

The speed at which computer technology is developing inevitably means that what I write will be out of date even before it's committed to print. Recent years have seen both a decline in the price and a rise in the power of personal computers. You can get a fairly basic word-processing kit, including a monochrome monitor, dot matrix printer and word-processing software, for around £400; Whereas £1,500 would buy you a powerful and sophisticated IBM-compatible personal computer (PC) with a built-in integrated suite of software (word processing, database, spreadsheet, graphics, communications, etc.), DOS and Windows operating systems, colour monitor and a bubblejet printer.

There may be a temptation for a community information service to assume that a computer is now a necessity for its work, before asking the obvious question: 'What do we need one for?' If an information service only wants a computer for maintaining its database, and that database is simple and relatively small, it may well find that one of the manual systems described in Chapter Four is quicker and more user-friendly. Consideration also needs to be given to the question of who is expected to use the computer. If your service relies on volunteers, they may have an aversion to new technology or simply not work long enough to become familiar with and confident in using a computer.

Before plunging into the murky waters of information technology (IT), you should first of all ask the kind of basic questions that needed to be addressed when setting up your service, such as 'Why do we need IT?', 'What functions do we want it to perform?', 'What system is going to meet our needs?', 'Who is going to use the system?', 'Where can I get advice?', 'What training will be required?', and so on.

There are many reasons why an information service might want a computer but they may not necessarily all be the right reasons. Some wrong reasons are:

- everybody else has got one;
- to improve the image of the service;
- to sort out our database/statistics/financial accounts, which are in a mess.

This latter brings to mind the computer cliché 'garbage in, garbage out', namely that if you put rubbish into a computer, you can expect to get rubbish out. Before inputting any information into a computer, you must first have a logical and organized manual system. The computer won't do it for you.

Some right reasons might be:

- to provide faster and more timely access to information;
- to facilitate access to a wider range of information;
- to provide more sophisticated access to information;
- to enable more people to have direct access to information.

Before making a decision on what equipment to purchase, consider what functions you want the computer to perform. These might be one or several of the following:

- *database management*;
- recording *statistics* and, possibly, producing these in graphic form, i.e. as bar or pie charts, graphs, etc.;
- running *welfare benefits* and other programs;
- running a local *viewdata* system;
- *online access* to other external databases;
- *word processing*;
- *financial accounting*;
- *desktop publishing*.

If you require most of these functions, a fairly powerful machine would be necessary but you might be better advised to consider more than one computer or even linking them in a *local area network* (LAN). A LAN enables personal computers to communicate with each other and share resources such as software and printers. Usually, a LAN is driven by a computer with a large hard disk which contains the software programs and the data input by the rest of the PCs or terminals on the system. It also provides access to shared printers on the network and to central back-up facilities.

Choosing the right equipment and software

There are several ways in which you might set about choosing a computer, depending on the level of knowledge of staff in your organization. Let us assume elementary or no knowledge of computers, in which case the options might be the following:

- *Dealers* – may be OK if you know one who can be trusted or is recommended, but computer salesmen, like car salesmen, frequently try to get you to buy a machine of a higher specification than you need and blind you with technical jargon. Also limits your ability to shop around.
- *Consultants* – usually expensive unless you can beg or borrow their services. Have a tendency to recommend separate software packages for each function or even writing a program to match needs exactly, rather than considering integrated packages which may require some compromise. OK if all the separate parts can work or are not required to work together.
- *Other organizations* in the same sector who use computers in their work may be able to recommend equipment and software from their own experience. However, they may be reluctant to admit shortcomings and the equipment/software they use may be out of date, given the speed of developments in this area.
- *Networks* who support advice services or community and voluntary organizations, such as Community Computing Network (65 Litchfield Road, Cambridge CB1 3SP) or the Computer Development Unit of LASA (2nd Floor, Universal House, Wentworth Street, London E1 7SA Tel. 071-377 2798). Apart from giving direct advice themselves, they may be able to put you in touch with others who can help.

Within the space of this book, it is not possible to consider all the potential uses to which a community information service may wish to put a computer. I have therefore concentrated on those aspects which, though not peculiar to information services, are a major feature of their work, namely database management (including viewdata and access to external databases), welfare benefits programs and enquiry statistics.

Database management

There are a number of reasons why a community information service would want to keep its information file on computer:

- beyond a certain point, a manual information file becomes unwieldy to use and update, whereas a computer database offers speed of access and ease of updating;
- complex searches involving, for example, subject, place and clientele, are extremely difficult and well nigh impossible to carry out with a manual system. A good computer database management system allows searching of the database by a combination of terms;
- individual records or subsets of the database can be printed out on demand in a variety of formats, e.g. as mailing labels, lists, standard letters;
- through networking, online or exchange of disks a computer database can be shared with other workers or organizations;
- customers can be given direct access to the database through public access terminals in your centre(s) or through a viewdata system (see below);
- entries can be fed into a word-processing or desktop publishing package and printed out as leaflets, directories, handbooks, etc. either directly or, more usually, by preparing a master copy which is then printed by offset litho.

A computer database is made up of two parts – the software, sometimes referred to as DBMS (database management system) and the database file, which is very much like a manual card index system in that it contains individual records made up of a number of fields (e.g. name, address, telephone number, hours of opening, etc.), into which bits of information (data) are entered (input). Most database systems store data in a highly structured form but there are some exceptions, known as free-form or text-retrieval databases, which automatically index all significant words in a document.

Some database systems allow information to be viewed or edited either in tabular form, with each record represented by a row and fields as columns, or a record at a time. The tabular approach is fine if the fields in each record are short but is less convenient where you have lengthy fields. This can usually be circumvented by limiting the number of characters in each field, but then you cannot see the record as a whole.

143

There are basically two types of database management systems: a *simple* DBMS produces a single file (sometimes called *flat file*) of records that have a predetermined number of fields and field lengths. This does not mean that field lengths cannot be varied or fields added or deleted, but any changes affect all the records in the file. A flat file may be adequate, say, for a database of community organizations, provided you have reasonably anticipated all the fields and field lengths that you are likely to require. However, it will not be suitable for a situation where you want to create several different files and have the ability to link them. For example, in addition to the database of community organizations, you may want databases of leaflets, booklets and pamphlets; 'hard' information; individuals who can provide help; and enquiries plus the ability to search on all of them simultaneously. In those circumstances, you are more likely to need a *relational* DBMS, which would enable you to form links between the different files through the use of common denominators, such as subject or classification fields, client reference number, etc.

Examples of flat file systems are Cardbox Plus (used by Help for Health for its database), Q&A, and FileMaker Pro. Most database functions that come as part of a suite of integrated software, such as LotusWorks, will be flat file systems and may not be sophisticated enough to cope with anything but a simple database. Some of the leading relational systems are DataEase, Paradox, and dBase systems (dBase IV, FoxPro, Clipper). I have used for a number of years a system called Superfile which, at the time, had the advantage of not requiring any programming knowledge from the user. However, most of the database systems have become more user-friendly over the years.

The price you can expect to pay for a DBMS can range from £250 to £750 but some suppliers offer substantial discounts to voluntary organizations and charities.

Choosing the software

Before choosing a database management system, you should first of all draw up a shopping list of requirements and questions that you need to ask, such as the following:

● Is there a maximum size of file that the system can handle? In most cases this will depend on the size of your computer's memory but some systems may operate more slowly as the database grows beyond a certain size.

● Is there any limit on the size of records, the number of fields in a record, or the size of a field? If so, is this likely to be a problem?

● Is it possible to add, expand or delete fields from a record without difficulty?

● Is it possible to print out all or a selection of records and fields within records in a structured format?

● Can the data be fed into other software packages to produce lists, standard letters, mailing labels, etc.?

● What features does the system provide for searching records? For example, wildcards (* ? =) are a means of truncating search terms to take account of varying forms or spelling, e.g. ORGAN* will find any first word in a field beginning with the letters O R G A N, such as 'organize', 'organization' etc.; 'sounds like' will find records with similar sounding words to the search term, e.g. FAIR and FARE; or Boolean logic will logically link or exclude terms to narrow the field of search, e.g. A and B, A or B, A-G but not C, etc.

● Is there a facility to check on the validity of entered data?

● Is there provision for constructing user-friendly menus?

● How much knowledge is required to set up a database? How long does it take to acquire that knowledge? Can it be self-taught?

● How good is the documentation that accompanies the system?

● Is there a multi-user version of the software?

● What support is offered by the supplier? Is there a user group?

Creating a database

Having bought your software and installed it on the computer, the next step is to create the database(s). Each database management system will have its own methods for setting up the database and this section can give only a few tips from experience that should apply to whatever system you have chosen.

First determine a *structure* for your database. If you are moving from a manual database, that structure may already exist. The method of determining a structure for a database is similar to that for a manual system, as set down in Chapter Four. However, in addition to identifying what fields you require, you will also need to determine field lengths. Be generous, if your system will allow, so that you are not continually changing field lengths.

Separate fields will need to be given *field names* or *tags* to which the computer attributes information that is being input. For example, you might decide to call the 'organization' field ORG and the 'address' field AD. Where a field consists of several lines, such as an address, it is advisable to split these into separate fields, particularly if you want to search on individual elements of an address field or to print them out as separate lines. An address field might thus be divided into two or three separate fields for building/house name, street, community/neighbourhood/village and fields for town, county and postcode. So your tags might look like AD1, AD2, COM, TOWN, COUNTY, PCODE. In some cases, a record might contain several repetitions of the same field types, e.g. names and addresses. Every time these occur you could give them the same tags, but this may cause problems when conducting searches or printing out information. For example, if you wanted to see or print out a list of organizations in, for example, the 'Parkside' neighbourhood, the computer would also throw up records for, say, the secretary or second contact who lives in the 'Parkside' neighbourhood, if they all have the tag COM. The simplest way to get round this is to add to the root name for tags a separate number for each occurrence within your record structure, e.g. COM1, COM2, COM3, etc.

There are occasions when it is advantageous to use the same tag for several fields:

1 You might, for instance, want to have several fields for subject headings. By giving them the same tag name, this will ensure that, in whatever subject field a particular term is entered, the computer will throw up the record when a search is made under that term. It will also ensure that when records are printed out, the record will appear under each subject heading.

2 When you want to link files in a relational database system, this can be achieved by having a field with the same tag name appearing in each file, e.g. subject, name of organization, client, etc. A search on that particular field will throw up records in all the files bearing the term entered.

It is advisable to have the database form in the same order as the form that you send out to organizations for their information, as this makes it easier for the person inputting the information.

See Figure 28 for an example of a computer database form.

```
CM131M          Cambridgeshire Libraries Community Information
                         Create Organisation
Record no.   :                              Last checked :
Organisation : _____

Addr: _____      Venue: _____
      _____             _____
Town: _____      Town: _____
Cnty: _____  P/Code: _____    Cnty: _____  P/Code: _____
Tele: _____
      First Contact                            Second Contact
Titl: ____                               Titl: ____
Fnme: _____      Fnme: _____
Snme: _____      Snme: _____
Posn: _____      Posn: _____
Addr: _____      Addr: _____
      _____             _____
Town: _____      Town: _____
Cnty: _____  P/Code: _____    Cnty: _____  P/Code: _____
Tel1: _____ (Home)         Tel1: _____ (Home)
Tel2: _____ (Bus)          Tel2: _____ (Bus)
```

```
CM132M          Cambridgeshire Libraries Community Information
                         Create Organisation
Org. Name :

Service    : _____
Desc         _____
             _____
             _____
             _____
             _____
             _____
             _____

Hours      : _____
             _____

Remarks    : _____
```

```
CM133M          Cambridgeshire Libraries Community Information
                         Create Organisation
Org. Name :

Subject    : _____    _____
Names        _____    _____
             _____    _____
             _____    _____
             _____    _____

Clientele : _____    _____
             _____    _____

Area Name : _____    _____
             _____    _____

Geographic: _____  _____    _____  _____
Codes        _____
```

/Continued overleaf

```
CM134M01        Cambridgeshire Libraries Community Information
                             Create Organisation

Org. Name :

Lib Class :  _____    _____
Codes        _____    _____
             _____    _____
             _____    _____
             _____    _____

AGM       :  __
Age Group :  __ ˉ __
Pub. Codes:  ____   ____

Entry Date:          Last Updated :          Last Checked :

```

Fig. 28 Cambridgeshire Libraries Community Information mainframe database – input screens.

One of the advantages of having a computerized database is that it enables you to *automate* administrative processes. For example, update letters can be customized and printed out as you determine (Figure 29). If you want to update continually throughout the year rather than in one session, then you will need to build into your record structure a field that enables you to do this, e.g. date record last updated or added, AGM date. Dates must be entered in a consistent form. Alternatively, you could update a section of the file each month by the initial letter of each organization, e.g. Month 1: A–B, Month 2: C–D, and so on.

When sending out update letters or forms for information about new organizations, if people's names and addresses are going to be recorded, make sure that you conform to the requirements of the Data Protection legislation by including a statement to the effect that: 'This information is being stored on a computer. Please indicate any items of information that you do not wish to be recorded.' Details of the Data Protection legislation are available in a series of free booklets from the Office of the Data Protection Registrar, Springfield House, Water Lane, Wilmslow, Cheshire SK9 5AX (Tel. 0625 535777.

When sending out an update letter, it is also helpful to send a printout of the organization's current entry as a prompt for any changes that may have occurred and to save the secretary time in filling out information that has not changed.

&TITLE& &INITIAL& &SNAME&
&ADDRESS1&
&ADDRESS2&
&ADDRESS3&
&PCODE&

[date]

Dear Sir/Madam,

&SOCIETY&

I understand that you are or were recently associated with the above group. I am enclosing a print-out of the entry in our files for the group. If there have been any changes to this information or not, I would be grateful if you would indicate this on the entry or on a separate sheet, and return it to me as soon as possible, so that we can update our files.

Under the provisions of the Data Protection Act, I have to inform you that this information is being stored on a computer. It will be used for answering enquiries received in the Reference Library by post, telephone or in person. Some of the information may be used in published information lists or directories. The information is also made available to other information and advice agencies and commercial organisations on request. **If there is any information that you do not wish to be stored on our computer files, would you please indicate this on the enclosed entry.**

Thank you for your help.

Yours sincerely,

Fig. 29 Cambridgeshire Libraries Community Information – update letter showing field tag names from database.

All database systems will have some facility for *sorting* records according to predetermined parameters, e.g. alphabetical by subject, then alphabetical by name of organization or by date, record number, place, etc. You can usually set up several sort codes for different purposes. The sorting facility is used mainly as a prerequisite when printing out records as a list. For this, you will use another element of a database management system, the *report* function (name may vary according to DBMS used). This enables you to print out information in a predetermined format, using all or a selection of fields in a record. Again, more than one report can be set up to take account

149

of different uses. In some integrated packages, the database records have to be fed into the word-processing package for printing out.

Uses of the database

You will need to consider potential uses of the database. Is it a tool for the staff alone to use in answering enquiries? Are you going to allow public access to records either as printouts or through an online terminal? Are you going to make the database available to other organizations through exchange of disks or even sell it to interested parties? The answers to some of these questions will have implications for the kind of hardware and software you choose, and therefore need to be decided at an early stage. For example, if you decide to allow public access via an online terminal, apart from the additional terminal and keyboard you will also need a multi-user version of the software which must be capable of building in safeguards to prevent the public either accidentally or deliberately erasing or changing records.

Some database systems offer *runtime* versions of the software at a substantially lower price. These allow the system to be run but cannot be used to make changes to it or to develop something new. A good example of this is Help for Health's Cardbox database, where subscribers receive a runtime version of Cardbox and regular updated disks of the database. Obviously, a runtime database will not be as up to date as a true online system but could be a cheaper and safer alternative.

You can also get *videotext* packages which run on PCs and enable you to marry attractive graphics with a database. A good example is the TAP (Training Access Point) terminals located in various public buildings to dispense information on training opportunities, both local and national. The national information was obtained through online links with remote databases. The local information database is maintained on a master PC and then transferred by disk at regular intervals to the PCs driving the TAP terminals. The advantages of this kind of system are:

- eye-catching graphics can be used to overcome the public's reluctance to use computers;
- protects your main database;
- less staff-intensive.

The disadvantages are:

- the information is not as up to date as a true online system;
- a PC is occupied just in running that function;
- it can become monopolized by young people who think it's the latest arcade game;
- if a printout facility is offered, this can easily be abused, requiring frequent staff attention;
- there is a need to make the equipment inaccessible or tamper-proof.

PC-based videotext terminals have been used to good effect by some commercial organizations to provide local information and advertising. You find these most often in the windows of tourist information centres, the computer display being operated by a touch-sensitive keypad attached to the window.

Another variation is to get a graphics package, such as Animator, which has the facility of enabling the computer to rotate a series of frames of information at set intervals. Several years ago COIC (Careers & Occupational Information Centre) offered a videotext package called Rotaview which enabled users to create colourful graphics and link these with a database. The system was used to prepare an offline database, to access or download frames of information from Prestel (see below), or to operate as a mini-viewdata service with users dialling into the database for information. Another attraction of Rotaview was its carousel feature that enabled up to 80 frames of information to be scrolled at intervals. A particular use for this type of feature in an information centre would be to display essential information to the public out of hours. Rotaview was marketed at schools, colleges and public libraries but, alas, was developed only for the BBC micro and is no longer available. However, with infinitely more powerful PCs around today, there must be similar software on the market, if you are interested in this way of displaying information.

Other database systems
Using a PC is not the only way of setting up a community information database. There are other options which may be open to services which are part of a much larger organization, like public libraries, and are designed to cope with extremely large databases and/or allow wider access.

In the early 1970s British Telecom (or The Post Office as it then was) developed a *viewdata* system called Prestel which enabled users to access thousands of pages of information on all sorts of topics via the medium of the telephone and specially adapted television sets (and later also PCs). The system has never quite lived up to its early promises but is still going strong. A number of public libraries were involved in the early trial of Prestel and recognized the potential of the system, if not of Prestel itself. Eventually, local authorities began to set up their own viewdata systems of information about council services and other local information. The public could access the system either directly from home or through terminals located in libraries and other public buildings. In some instances, the library service is responsible for maintaining the database, in others another department of the local authority. Viewdata systems offer the following:

- access to large amounts of continually updated information;
- use of graphics;
- public online access from home, workplace or publicly located terminals;
- centralized updating of information.

Some disadvantages are:

- they need dedicated teams to maintain the database;
- many clientele of community information services would not be able to afford equipment to access the database or would be afraid of using a computer;
- limitations on the amount of information that can reasonably be presented by the system.

A good example of a viewdata system can be found in the following article:

Baker, Patrick, 'Themis at your service', *Public library journal*, **3** (3), 1988, 62–3.

Some public libraries, like Berkshire, are beginning to recognise the income-generating potential of viewdata, with electronic *Yellow pages*, teleshopping, rental pages, and closed user group facilities. For more details see:

Hicks, John, 'Viewdata: the income generation game', *Aslib information*, May 1988, 119–20.

Further information on the use of viewdata for community information will be found in:

Library operations checklist No. 9 Community videotex (viewdata) to network local community information, Public Libraries Group, 1988, £1.75.

Apart from running viewdata systems, mini- or mainframe computers can also be the hosts for community information databases using such software as IBM's STAIRS (Storage and Information Retrieval System). Some libraries set up their databases on a mainframe computer from the start; others, like my own, have transferred from a PC-based system. Some advantages of using a mainframe computer are:

● almost limitless power;
● speed of operation;
● updating from multi-access points;
● online access from other council departments, the public, etc.;
● possible links into computer issue systems;
● feedback from other departments/organizations using the system.

Disadvantages are:

● they are not particularly user-friendly – no use of graphics;
● it can be difficult to maintain consistency of input and updating with multi-access;
● they take second place to other council programmes, such as payroll.
● you need to 'log on' each time the system is used.

A good example of a mainframe-driven community information system is Cheshire's CHIPS, which you can read about in:

Benton, Raymond and Peacock, Alan, 'CHIPS with everything: automated community information in Cheshire', *Library Association record*, **90** (11), 1988, 665–6.

Reference was made above to possible links between mainframe-based community information files and library computerized issue systems. In fact, a number of these systems now offer add-on features for storing community information themselves. The advantages of these are:

- access to database through every library in the system;
- public access through OPACs (Online Public Access Terminals) or, in some cases, dial-in facilities;
- multi-access to inputting and updating database.

Disadvantages are:

- they can slow down issue system;
- they are not usually accessible by other council departments;
- with multi-access, it can be difficult to maintain consistency of inputting and updating;
- as with viewdata systems, information is usually limited.

Inevitably, with a technology that is developing so fast, there will be new systems for presenting information coming along. Glasgow has been experimenting with HyperCard, which allows the user to search through text, pictures, numbers and instructions to gain information about the city. Before long someone is bound to be using CD-ROM or interactive video.

Online searching
Another use for your PC might be to link into other remote databases, such as a local authority's viewdata system. To do this you will need a *modem*, to link the PC to the telephone network, and communications software, which could be a separate package or part of a suite of software such as LotusWorks or Windows 3. When buying equipment and software seek advice from the same sources listed on p. 142 above. Most online databases, except for local viewdata, are not appropriate for community information services, but there is one that is: *Volnet UK*, operated jointly by The Volunteer Centre UK and the Community Development Foundation. Volnet UK is an online information service containing thousands of references to press items, journal articles, reports, books and current research projects on community development, voluntary action, youth affairs, child care and social policy issues, stored on an easy-to-use computer database. For a modest annual fee (£30 local community/voluntary agency, £90 national/regional voluntary agency, £150 central/local government department) you get unlimited access to the database (no charge per second or minute), a telephone helpline, plus a photocopy service for articles, for which a small charge is made. Details from Volnet UK, Community Development Foundation, 60 Highbury Grove, London N5 2AG (Tel. 071-226 5375).

Computer programs

Welfare benefits

Providing welfare benefits information and advice can be notoriously difficult because of the complex legislation, which is why some advice centres and public library community information services are harnessing the power of PCs to help them. These are usually designed for use by advisers although, over the years, some attempt has been made to develop client-operated systems, largely without success.

Welfare benefits programs contain the rules of the benefits system and present on the computer screen a series of questions. The adviser, in consultation with the client, types in the details and the computer works out whether the client is entitled to benefit and, if so, how much. The results can usually be printed out and given to the client to take away. The main benefits covered include Income Support, Housing Benefit, Family Credit and Community Charge Benefit. The advantages of these programs are:

- consistency;
- they do not let you forget little-used regulations or 'passport' benefits, where claiming one benefit automatically entitles the client to others;
- a novice worker can tackle more complex cases;
- 'what-if' calculations can be done speedily;
- printouts of results can be obtained;
- some clients like the computerized approach and are reassured by it.

Some disadvantages are:

- they are only as accurate as the information input;
- the benefits system is so complex, programs are bound to have quirks;
- an experienced adviser can usually work faster than the program;
- they can lead to over-confidence;
- some clients can be intimidated by a computer and find it intrusive;
- they are no substitute for experience.

The following chart (Figure 30) lists the main welfare benefits programs available and their features. For more details, addresses,

155

Supplier	Product	Benefits covered *			Computers provided for				Cost (£)	
		Basic	NC	Cont.	H-held	PC	PCW	Other	New	P.a.
Roy Bailey	Evesham Benefits Program	✓			✓	✓			100	50
Bath Computing	Benefactor	✓				✓		✓	300	270
Ferret	Maximiser Plus	✓	✓	✓		✓		✓	100	111
	Helper-Plus	✓	DWA		✓				165	73
	In-work Helper	✓	DWA		✓				215	84
ICL (UK)	Welfare Benefits Adviser	✓	✓			✓		✓	1200	250
Inside Communications	Bene	✓			✓				85	25
Lisson Grove	Lisson Grove Welfare Benefits Advice Prog	✓	✓	✓		✓				60

* Benefits:"Basic" = Income Support, Housing Benefit, Family Credit, Community Charge Benefit
"NC" = many or all non-contributory benefits
"Cont." = advice/information on likely contributory benefits

**Fig. 30 Welfare benefits programs available May 1992. From: *Compu-
tanews factsheet: welfare benefits programs*, London Advice
Services Alliance, 1992, 3.**

etc., see the *Computanews* factsheet *Welfare benefits programs* (see
below for details of all the factsheets in this series).

Although ten years old now, there is still value in consulting the
following seminal report:

Ottley, Pennie and Kempson, Elaine, *Computer benefits? Guidelines
for local information and advice centres*, National Consumer
Council, 1982.

Other programs
There are other PC-based programs and databases available on such
areas as debt advice calculations and sources of funding from
charitable trusts. Resource Information Services (RIS – Tel. 071-494
2408), in conjunction with LASA's Computer Development Unit, is
currently developing a database of advice agencies in London for
piloting in autumn 1992. A good way of keeping up with the latest
developments in programs for advice work is to take out a
subscription to the excellent bimonthly periodical *Computanews*
(details below).

Statistics

Collating and manipulating statistics is one area where computers have a distinct advantage. They can do in seconds or minutes what would take hours of work manually. However, if all you want the computer to do is add up and produce totals in broad categories, then you might as well stick to pencil and calculator. But, for detailed analysis of enquiries and graphic representation of information by means of pie or bar charts, graphs, etc., you will need a computer program. There are two options: either devise your own system using a spreadsheet package or a relational database system linked with a spreadsheet package, or buy a specially designed program. A lot of the pioneer work in this field has been carried out by LASA's Computer Development Unit which, some years ago, developed CRESS (Client Records and Enquiry Statistics Service) and is currently engaged on developing a model recording system called STATS (see p. 134).

Finally, there are many more uses to which a community information service might wish to put its computer, e.g. word processing, accounts, graphics, desktop publishing, but these aspects apply to many other organizations and it is beyond the scope of this book to cover them. More details of these and other aspects will be found in an excellent series of *Computanews factsheets* produced by the Computer Development Unit of LASA. These cost £3.00 each or £20.00 for the full set and cover *Buying a computer, Desk-top publishing, Databases, Printers, Networks, Word processing, Health & safety, Spreadsheets, Accounts programs,* and *Welfare benefits programs*. They are written in layperson's language and offer sensible, down-to-earth advice as well as names and addresses of suppliers, manufacturers, etc.

A subscription to *Computanews* (bimonthly, £12.00 voluntary organizations, £20.00 others) is well worth it for the cartoons alone!

LASA's Computer Development Unit can be found at 2nd Floor, Universal House, 88–94 Wentworth Street, London E1 7SA (Tel. 071-377 2798.

Further reading

Press enter: information technology in the community and voluntary sector, Community Development Foundation, 1992, £4.95 + 50p p&p.

Further reading

Bunch, Allan, *Community information services: the origin, scope and development*, Clive Bingley, 1982, £20.00.

Informing communities: the role of libraries and information services, ed. by Margaret Kinnell, Community Services Group of the Library Association, 1992, £20.00.

Matthews, Howard, *Community information: a manual for beginners*, Association of Assistant Librarians, 1988.

Thornton, Christine, *Managing to advise*, Federation of Independent Advice Centres, 1989, £4.95.

Model job specification for the organizer of an information service

Numbers in brackets refer to notes at the end of the specification.

Function: To provide ... (1) ... with ... (2) ... to enable them to ... (3) ... This is to be achieved through the organization of ... (4) ... designed to meet the needs of the community.

Responsibility: The organizer is responsible to ... (5).

Specific duties and responsibilities:
1 *Staff*
   The organizer is responsible for
● the recruitment and selection of suitable paid and/or voluntary staff to operate the service;
● ensuring that all staff receive initial and ongoing training;
● assessing the performance of all staff and, where necessary, recommending appropriate action to ... (5);
● arranging effective communication with staff through regular meetings, staff bulletins, etc.;
● providing advice and support to all staff.

2 *Administration*
   The organizer is responsible for
● establishing and maintaining an up-to-date and accurate information system to meet the needs of users and staff of the service;
● keeping adequate records relating to the use of the service;
● handling correspondence;
● maintaining an adequate supply of stationery and other items;
● keeping financial records relating to the sale of items by the service and the disbursement of petty cash;

- dealing with complaints against the service;
- the security of the premises.

3 *Liaison and public relations*
The organizer is responsible for
- developing links with local, regional and national agencies and individuals whose work or knowledge might be of benefit to the service;
- representing the service on any appropriate bodies, committees, etc.;
- publicizing and promoting the service through all appropriate channels;
- drawing attention to local issues or shortcomings arising out of the work of the service;
- preparing an annual report.

4 *Finance*
The organizer, with ... (6) ..., is responsible for the preparation of estimates, applications for grants and the budget.

5 *Development*
The organizer is responsible, with the help of ... (5) ..., for
- the continual monitoring of the use made of the service and for recommending any alterations to improve the service or meet changing needs;
- the development of additional services within the centre considered necessary to meet the needs of users or potential users;
- the development of any external sessions or extensions of the service deemed to be necessary.

Notes
1 Statement of clientele, e.g. the general public, members of a particular organization, residents on a certain estate, etc.

2 Statement about the kind of service to be offered, e.g. information, advice, support, etc.

3 Statement of purpose for which the service is being provided, e.g. to enable people to obtain their rights, to improve decision making, to help solve everyday problems, etc.

4 Statement of type of organization, e.g. information service, sup-

port unit, current awareness service, etc.

5 Statement of body or person ultimately responsible for the service to whom the organizer reports e.g. management committee, librarian, administrative officer, etc.

6 Statement of any body or person responsible for the financial control of the service, e.g. treasurer, librarian, finance officer, finance subcommittee, etc.

This job specification is based on that drawn up by the the National Association of Citizens' Advice Bureaux for Bureau Organizer, with deletions, amendments and additions of my own in order to make it more generally applicable. Not all the responsibilities listed above will be appropriate to every type of service, so you will need to select from or add to this model in the light of your own circumstances.

List of umbrella organizations covering community information and advice services

Advice and information services in general
Advice Services Alliance, c/o LASA, 2nd Floor, Universal House, 88–94 Wentworth Street, London E1 7SA (Tel. 071-377 2798).
London Advice Services Alliance (LASA), 2nd Floor, Universal House, 88–94 Wentworth Street, London E1 7SA (Tel. 071-377 2798.

Citizens advice bureaux
National Association of Citizens' Advice Bureaux, Myddelton House, 115–123 Pentonville Road, London N1 9LZ (Tel. 071-833 2181).
Citizens Advice Scotland, 26 George Square, Edinburgh, Scotland EH8 9LD (Tel. 031-664 0156).

Community organizations and workers
National Council for Voluntary Organizations, Regent's Wharf, 8 All Saints Street, London N1 9RL (Tel. 071-713 6161).
National Federation of Community Organizations, 8/9 Upper Street, London N1 0PQ (Tel. 071-226 0189).
Northern Ireland Council for Voluntary Action, 127 Ormeau Road, Belfast BT7 1SH (Tel. 0232 321224).
Scottish Council for Voluntary Organisations, 18–19 Claremont Crescent, Edinburgh EH7 4QD (Tel. 031-556 3882).
Wales Council for Voluntary Action, Llys Ifor, Heol Crescent, Caerffili, Canoi Morgannwyg CF8 1XL (Tel. 0222 869224/5/6).

Disabled information and advice lines
DIAL UK, Park Lodge, St Catherine's Hospital, Thickhill Road, Balby, Doncaster DN4 8QN (Tel. 0302 310123).

Elderly information and advice services
Age Concern England, Astral House, 1268 London Road, London
   SW16 4EJ (Tel. 081-679 8000).

Housing advice centres
Shelter, 88 Old Street, London EC1V 9AX (Tel. 071-253 0202).

Independent/neighbourhood advice centres
Federation of Independent Advice Centres, Concourse House, Lime
   Street, Liverpool L1 1NY (Tel. 051-709 7444) – national office;
   13 Stockwell Road, London SW9 9AU (Tel. 071-274 1839) –
   London unit.

Legal advice and law centres
Law Centres Federation, Duchess House, 18–19 Warren Street,
   London W1P 5DB (Tel. 071-387 8368).

Money advice centres
Money Advice Association, Aizlewoods Mill, Nursery Street,
   Sheffield S3 8GG (Tel. 0742 823165).
Money Advice Scotland, 43 Broughton Street, Edinburgh, Scotland
   (Tel. 031-557 6149).

Youth counselling, advice and information centres
Youth Access, Magazine Business Centre, 11 Newarke Street,
   Leicester LE1 5GS (Tel. 0533 558763).

Adirondack, Sandy, *Just about managing* 48

Audio-visual guide for community groups 126

Baker, Patrick, 'Themis at your service' 152

Beal, Christina, *Community profiling* 10

Benton, Raymond and Peacock, Alan, 'CHIPS with everything' 153

Brake, Terence, *The need to know* 7

British Library Research & Development Department, *Priorities for research 1989–1994* 27

Bunch, Allan and Hemmings, Richard, 'Umbrella groups' 14

Callaghan, J. and Yeomans, K., *Local radio kit* 126

Callaghan, John, *Costing for contracts* 22

The central government grants guide 24

Clarke, Sam, *The complete fundraising handbook* 26

'Community analysis and libraries' 10

Community information: what libraries can do viii

Computanews 157

Computanews factsheets 157

Consumer Congress directory 12

Conway, Lisa, *Training* 54

Corporate citizen 25

Counselling & psychotherapy resources directory 12

Darvill, Giles, *The impact of contracts on volunteers* 48

Davison, Ann and Seary, Bill, *Grants from Europe* 26

Designing a community information system 83

Directory enquiries 106

Directory of educational guidance services 12

Directory of grant-making trusts 24

Directory of independent advice services 12

Directory of Social Change fundraising leaflets 26

Directory of Welsh consumer organizations 12

Disability rights handbook 12

Doyle, Matt and Mocroft, Ian, *Working it out* 15

Drinkwater, Jane, *Get it on...radio and television* 126

Edwards, Ken, *Contracts in practice* 22

English Tourist Board, *How can I help you?* 87

Environmental grants 26

Essentials of health and safety at work 55

Evaluation and monitoring in voluntary organizations 139

Feek, W., *Working effectively* 139

Ford, C. and Silley, A., *Insurance protection* 55

Ford, Jane and Merriman, Philippa, *The gentle art of listening* 54

Getting the message across 106
Going for advice 11
A guide to company giving 25
A guide to the major trusts 24
Hawley, Keith, *From grants to contracts* 22
Hicks, John 'Viewdata: the income generation game' 153
HIV & AIDS: a funding guide... 26
Holloway, Christine and Otto, Shirley, *Getting organised* 48
Holman, Kay, 'Holding the umbrella' 14
Humble, Stephen, *High Street giving* 25
Jones, Clara S., *Public library information and referral service* 50
Jones, M., *Government grants* 24
Jones, Maggie, *Using the media* 126
Jordan, Peter and Whalley, E.D., *Learning about the community* 10
King, Ivan, *Promote!* 127
King, Stephen, *Display screen equipment* 55
Kinnell, Margaret, *Planned public relations for libraries* 127
Kirby, John, *Creating the library indentity* 115
Lawrie, Alan, *Quality of service* 139
Library operations checklist No. 3 Compiling a community profile 10
Library operations checklist No. 9 Using videotex ... 153
Line, Maurice, *Library surveys* 8
The London grants guide 26
Lowndes, Barbara, *Getting your message across* 127
MacIntosh, Dorothy and Alastair, *A basic PR guide* 127
The major companies guide 25

Matthews, Howard, *Community information* 77
Miles, John, *Design for desktop publishing* 128
Moore, Nick, *How to do research* 8, 137
National Council for One Parent Families, *Information manual* 95
Newspaper press directory 121
Norton, Michael, *How to write better fundraising applications* 26
Norton, Michael, *Raising money from industry* 25
Norton, Michael, *Raising money from trusts* 24
Ottley, Penny and Kempson, Elaine, *Computer benefits?* 156
Parker, Nicola, *Charities and broadcasting* 126
The Plain English story 8
Press enter: information technology in the community and voluntary sector 157
Printed reference material... 61, 74
Profiling the community 10
Pyle, John and Harrington, Simon, *Making leaflets work* 117
Quilliam, Susan and Stephenson, Ian Grove, *Into print...* 128
Quinn, Patrick, *Effective copy writing for librarians* 128
Radical bookseller 78
Reid, Julia M., *Education and training for community information and advice work* 50
Semple, Audrey, *Sell space to make money* 128
Step by step: a guide to volunteer fundraising 48
Supporting volunteers 48
Tackling training 54
Telephone helplines 33

Tourist information centres in Britain 12

Training to advise 54

Trust monitor 24

Turick, Dorothy, *Community information services in libraries* 50

Turner, Chris, *Organizing information* 83

User's guide to the media 126

Vaughan, Jenny, *Getting into print* 128

Voluntary but not amateur 48

Voluntary work in advice centres 48

Wasserman, Cressida, *Protecting volunteers* 55

The West Midlands grants guide 26

Whitcher, Angela, *All expenses paid?* 48

Whitcher, Angela, *Making the right choice* 49

Who knows?: guidelines for a review of local advice and information services... 11, 104, 106

Willings press guide 121

Woolf, Jo, *The beginner's guide to contracts* 22

Youth access referral directory 12

Zeitlyn, Jonathan, *Effective publicity and design* 128

accommodation
  local authority 22–3
Administrative, Professional,
    Technical & Clerical scales
  (APT&C) 46
advertising 127
  radio 123
  source of funding for directories
    102–3
advice 17
advice services
  space requirements 31
  staffing 45
advocacy
  functions of a community
    information service 17
  staffing 45
alphabetical arrangement 69–70
  of directories 106
Ansafones 33
arrangement
  alphabetical 69–70
  of directories 106
bookshelves 37
Bretton AID Centre, Peterborough
  enquiry record sheet 133
Bretton Township, Peterborough
  library survey 138
British Library Research &
    Development Department 27–8
businesses
  source of finance 25
CHIPS (Cheshire's computerized
    community information system)
  153
CRESS (Client Records and Enquiry

Statistics Service) 157
Cambridgeshire Libraries &
  Information Service 100
  community information database
    form 147–8; update letter 149
Camden Community Information
  Network Directory and
  Exchange (CINDEX) 99
Camden Free Leaflets Information
  Service 27, 28, 80
Cardbox 150
card drawers 34
card files
  equipment for community
    information service 33–6
cards
  for storing information 65–6
  stationery 41
chairs 31, 32
Child Poverty Action Group
  training courses 52
citizen's guides
  source of local information 60
Cambridgeshire Libraries
  community information
    classification scheme 82
classification 81–3
clubs and societies
  collecting information on 63
collecting local information 58–65
commercial organizations
  source of finance 24–5
community action
  functions of a community
    information service 18
  responsibilities of management

committee 20
Community Computing Network 142
community education
    functions of a community
        information service 17
community information
    definition viii
    joint collection of 14
    sharing 13
community information services
    directories of 13
    extending 13
    functions 16–19
    identifying existing services 11–12
    need for 1–15
    umbrella organizations 165–6
community newspapers
    use for publicity 119–20
community profiling 9–11
community service adverts 120
Computer Development Unit 142,
    156–7
community work courses 52
computer hardware
    choosing 142
computer networks
    support 142
computers 140–157
    equipment for community
        information service 33
    for storing information 66
    for keeping statistics 134
continuous learning 54
contracts
    staffing 47
co–operation 13
Councils for Voluntary Services
    directories as source of local
        information 60
counselling
    functions of a community
        information service 18
    staffing

counselling services
    space requirements 31
counting devices 130
current awareness
    bulletins 106–9
    services 17
database management 143–54
databases
    creating 145–50
Data Protection Act 62, 148
Data Protection Registrar 148
Datex Slipstrip index 40
day books
    enquiry statistics 131–2
deposit collections 93
deposit files 93–4
desktop publishing
    use in producing publications
        95–6
desks 31
directories
    source of local information 58–61
    use in disseminating information
        102–6
Directory of Social Change
    training courses 53
Disability Alliance
    training courses 52
display boards 38, 40
displays
    disseminating information 89–92
    publicity 117–19
dissemination of information 84–113
distribution
    of information leaflets 101
Donohue, Joseph C. viii
drawers 31
drop-in information centres 31
EEC (European Economic
        Community)
    source of finance 25–6
edge punched cards
    for storing information 65–6

employer's liability insurance 55
enquiries
   statistics 129–34
enquiry desk 31
enquiry forms 132–4
enquiry record sheets 130–1, 133
enquiry work
   by post 88–9
   by telephone 86–8
   face-to-face 84–6
entries
   in directories 104–6
ephemeral material
   organizing 80–1
Ethnic Minority Grant 23
European Economic Community
      (EEC)
   source of finance 25–6
European Social Fund 25
equipment 31–41
evaluation of information services
      129–39
exhibitions
   publicity 118
face-to-face enquiry work
   dissemination of information 84–6
Federation of Independent Advice
      Centres (FIAC)
   model statistical form 131
   training courses 52–3
feedback 134–5
field names 145–6
folders 41
files
   housekeeping 70–1
   organizations 67
   place 69
   subject 68–9
   updating 71–3
filing cabinets 36
filing systems 66–73
   letter by letter 69–70
   word by word 69–70

finance 21–9
flat file 144
format
   of directories 103
free material
   acquisition 79–80
Freephone services 33
funding
   for directories 102–3
fundraising guides 26
furniture and equipment 31–41
gate-keepers
   role in identifying information
      needs 3
   collecting information 58
government departments and
      agencies
   source of finance 23–4
grants 21–6
graphics 98–101
groups
   support 14
   umbrella 14
   use in identifying information
      needs 3
handbills
   publicity 116
handbooks
   use in disseminating information
      109–10
'hard' information 73–81
   acquisition 77–80
   framework for collecting 74–7
   organizing 80–1
headed paper 98
health and safety 54
Help for Health 150
helplines 33
housekeeping
   card files 70–1
Hypercard 154
income generation 28
   viewdata systems 152

indexes
  for directories 106
information
  joint collection 14
  sharing 13
information base 56–83
  coverage 56–7
  'hard' information 57, 73–81
  'soft' information 57–73
  supplementary information 57, 81
information files 66–73
information giving
  functions of a community
    information service 17
  space requirements 30
  staffing 45
information needs
  identifying 2–11
insurance 54–5
interviews
  monitoring use 136–7
  radio 122
issue systems
  computerized 153–4
job descriptions 43
job specification
  model 161–3
joint collection of information 13
Joint Council for the Welfare of
    Immigrants
  training courses 53
Kalamazoo strip indexes 40
LANs (local area networks) 141–2
LASA (London Advice Services
    Alliance)
  training courses 53
Lambeth Public Libraries 'Link'
    Service 20
leaflet racks and dispensers 37–8,
    39
leaflets
  acquisition 79–80
  publicity 116–17

organizing 80–1
  use in disseminating information
    98–101
lettering 101
librarianship courses 51–2
Library Association 52
Library Association Working Party
    on Community Information viii
lists
  for storing information 65
  for disseminating information
    97–9
Liverpool Business School
    Department of Information and
    Library Studies 51
lobbying
  responsibilities of management
    committee 20
local area networks 141–2
local authorities
  directories as source of local
    information 58
  premises 22–3
  source of finance 21–3
local information 17
location
  of community information service
    29
logos 98, 114–15
London Advice Services Alliance
    (LASA)
  model statistics recording system
    134
  training courses 53
London Borough Grants Scheme 23
loose-leaf binders 66
mainframe computers 153–4
management 19–20
management committees
  responsibilities 19–20
Manchester Polytechnic Department
    of Library and Information
    Studies 51

The media
  for transmitting information
    112–13
  publicity 119–23
meetings
  open 4–5
  publicity 4
  use in identifying information
    needs 3–5
  venue 4
microcomputers
  equipment for community
    information service 66
mini-computers 153–4
modems 154
monitoring use 129–39
  responsibilities of management
    committee 20
NACAB (National Association of
    Citizens Advice Bureaux)
  classification scheme 83
  information service 93–5
  income generation 28
  model job specification 161–3
NCOPF (National Council for One
    Parent Families) 95
NCVO (National Council for
    Voluntary Organisations)
  training courses 53
NJC (National Joint Council)
  conditions of service 46
name
  of information service 114–15
National Association of Citizens
    Advice Bureau
  classification scheme 83
  information service 93–5; income
    generation 28
  model job specification 161–3
National Consumer Council 104
National Council for One Parent
    Families (NCOPF) 95
National Council for Voluntary

Organisations (NCVO)
  training courses 53
National Joint Council (NJC)
  conditions of service 46
National Money Advice Training
    Unit 52
need for community information
    services 1–15
newspapers
  publicity 119–21
notepads 41
noticeboards
  community 92
  equipment for community
    information service 37
  use in disseminating information
    89–90
number tally machines 129–30
online searching 154
opening hours 43
order records 77–80
  free material 79–80
  priced publications 77–8
  periodicals 78–9
organizations file 67
outreach
  functions of a community
    information service 18
PLDIS (Public Library Development
    Incentive Scheme) 23, 26–7
packs
  training materials 53
  use in disseminating information
    110–12
pamphlet boxes 41
periodicals
  acquisition 78–9
person specification 43
Peterborough Council for Voluntary
    Service 108
Peterborough Information Group
    (PIG) 108, 115, 117–19
Peterborough Learning Centre 27

photocopiers
  colour 102
photographs
  publicity 118
place file 69
  postal enquiries 88–9
posters
  displaying 89–90
  publicity 115–16
  use in disseminating information
    101–2
practical help
  functions of a community
    information service 17
premises 29–31
  local authority 22–3
  shared 14
printing 96–7
The Press Association 121
press cuttings service 17
press releases 123–6
Prestel 152
professional indemnity insurance 55
promotion 114–28
publications
  acquisition 77–8
  criteria for selecting 76–7
  framework for collecting 74–6
  organizing 80–3
  use in disseminating information
    95–112
publicity 114–28
  support functions 17
public liability insurance 55
Public Library Development
    Incentive Scheme (PLDIS) 23,
    26–7
public service announcements
  radio and television 123
questionnaires
  for monitoring use 135–6
  use in identifying information
    needs 5–8

use in collecting local information
    62–4
radio
  use for publicity 121–3
  use for transmitting information
    112
reference books
  loan collections 17
referral
  functions of a community
    information service 17
refresher courses 54
relational database management
    systems 144
reports
  computer databases 149–50
research
  monitoring use 137
Rondex 35
Rondofile 34–5
Rotadex 36
Rotaview 151
rules
  for community information
    services 20
runtime database software 150
Rural Development Commission
  source of finance 23
Rural Social Partnership Fund 23
SDI (selective dissemination of
    information) 92–3
SHAC (Shelter Housing Action
    Centre)
  training courses 52
STAIRS (Storage and Information
    Retrieval System) 153
STATS model statistics recording
    system 134, 157
salaries 43, 46
self-help
  functions of a community
    information service 16
self-help services

space requirements 30
  staffing 44
selective dissemination of
    information (SDI) 17, 92–3
service conditions 46
services
  collecting information on 63–4
shared premises 14
sharing information 13
Shelter Housing Action Centre
    (SHAC)
  training courses 52
silk screen 102
'soft' information
  collecting 57–65
  filing system 66–73
  storage 65–66
software
  choosing 142
  database management systems
    144–5
sorting records
  computer databases 149
space requirements
  community information services
    30–1
South Hackney School 'The Need to
    Know' Project 5, 7, 27
South Molton Community
    Information Project 5–6
staffing 42–55
  activities 43–6
  contracts 47
  job descriptions 43
  numbers 43
  person specification 43
stationery 41
statistics
  computerized 157
  monitoring use 129–34
statistics sheets 41
Step One Help & Advice Centre,
    Peterborough 111

strip indexes
  equipment for community
    information service 40
  for storing information
structure
  of community information services
    19
subject files 68–9
subject headings 68
subject index 68
  in directories 106
supplementary information 81
support
  functions of a community
    information service 16–17
support groups 14
support services
  collecting information 58
  space requirements 30
  staffing 44
surveys
  for monitoring use 135–7
  use in identifying information
    needs 5–8
TAPS (Training Access Points)
    150
tags 145–6
talks
  publicity 126–7
telephone
  equipment 32–3
  use in collecting local information
    62
  use in enquiry work
television
  use for publicity 123
training 49–54
  community work courses 52
  continuous learning 53–4
  induction 49
  internal courses 49–50
  librarianship courses 51–2
  training packs 53

voluntary organizations' courses
52–3
Training Access Points 150
Training and Enterprise Councils
source of finance 23
trusts
source of finance 24
umbrella organizations
of community information services
14, 165–6
University of Central England in
Birmingham Faculty of
Computing and Information
Studies 52
University of Northumbria
Department of Information and
Library Management 51
University of Sheffield Department
of Information Studies 51
University of Wales Department of
Information and Library Studies
52
updating
card files 71–3
computer databases 148–9
VDUs (visual display units)
health and safety 54
videos

publicity 126
training materials 53
videotex 150–1
viewdata 152
visual display units (VDUs)
health and safety 54
Volnet UK 155
The Volunteer Centre UK
training courses 53
volunteers 47–9
recruiting 48
training 49–54
wallets
use for compiling packs of
information 112
welfare benefits
computer programs 155–6
Werrington District Library
Information Centre, Peterborough 31
window displays
use in disseminating information
91
word processing
for producing publications 95–6
Yellow pages
source of local information 58